COLETTE

In the same series:

Modern Literature Monographs

COLETTE

Robert D. Cottrell

Frederick Ungar Publishing Co.
New York

To Amelia

848.7
C82c
9/280
Jan. 1975

Contents

Chronology

1910:   Divorce from Willy. *La Vagabonde*. On December 2 began writing for *Le Matin*, whose editor-in-chief was Henry de Jouvenel.

1912:   Death of Sido (September 25). Marriage to Henry de Jouvenel (December 19).

1913:   Birth of daughter, Colette de Jouvenel (July 3). *L'Envers du music-hall. L'Entrave.*

1914–1918:   Journalism.

1916:   *La Paix chez les bêtes.*

1919:   *Mitsou*. Literary editor of *Le Matin*.

1920:   *Chéri*. Named "Chevalier de la Légion d'honneur."

1922:   *La Maison de Claudine.*

1923:   Acted in stage adaptation of *Chéri* at Nice and Marseille. *Le Blé en herbe*. Series of lectures in Midi. Separation from Henry de Jouvenel (December).

1924:   Left *Le Matin*. Wrote for *Le Figaro*.

1925:   Met Maurice Goudeket; beginning of their liaison. Divorce from Jouvenel.

1926:   Visit to Morocco with Goudeket. Bought "La Treille Muscate" in Saint-Tropez. Lecture tour in Switzerland. *La Fin de Chéri*.

1927:   Acted in stage adaptation of *La Vagabonde* in Paris.

1928:   *La Naissance du jour*. Named "Officier de la Légion d'honneur."

1929:   *La Seconde*. Visit to Spain and North Africa. Lecture tour in Germany.

1930:   *Sido*. Cruise in Norway. Goudeket gave up business and turned to journalism.

1931:   Lectured in Bucharest. Broke leg, probably one cause of arthritis later.

1932: *Ces plaisirs* (later entitled *Le Pur et l'impur*). Opened beauty salon in Paris. Lecture tour in France, Germany, Switzerland, Belgium.

1933: *La Chatte*. Drama critic for *Le Journal*.

1934: *Duo.*

1935: Marriage to Maurice Goudeket. Elected to the Belgian Royal Academy. On *The Normandy* for its maiden voyage. Brief stay in New York.

1936: *Mes Apprentissages.*

1938: Signs of arthritis.

1940: Left Paris during general wartime exodus in spring, but returned in September. Stayed in Paris during war.

1941: *Julie de Carneilhan. Journal à rebours.* Goudeket arrested by Nazis (December).

1942: Goudeket released. Paralyzed by arthritis. *De ma Fenêtre.*

1945: Elected to Goncourt Academy.

1946: *L'Étoile Vesper.*

1949: *Le Fanal bleu*. President of Goncourt Academy.

1949–1950: Publication of *Oeuvres complètes.*

1953: Named "Grand-officier de la Légion d'honneur."

1954: Died August 3. State funeral in the Cour d'honneur of the Palais-Royal. Buried in the Père-Lachaise cemetery in Paris.

The Beginning

The usual distinction between fiction and autobiography is inadequate when discussing Colette. Like Montaigne who was, or so he maintained, consubstantial with his *Essays*, Colette is pervasively and unremittingly present throughout her entire work. Yet, with the remarkable lucidity and detachment she always displayed when analyzing her own art, she affirmed, quite correctly, that her books would give but little information to a biographer. Singularly free from the compulsion to explain or justify her conduct, Colette, despite the autobiographical mode of much of her work, remains as mysteriously secretive, evasive and reticent as a cat, the animal from which she learned, so she says, the beauty and power of silence.

Eschewing the various literary fashions that came and went between 1900, the date of her first book, and 1949, the date of her last, Colette remained as remarkably faithful to her inner vision as she was to her famous frizzy hairdo which she adopted around 1902 and never abandoned (feeling somehow protected and less vulnerable behind the waves of hair that covered a forehead she thought too high, bold and masculine). In the last years of her life, she cast a backward glance from time to time over the many books she had written—some fifty volumes of novels, short stories, newspaper articles and drama reviews, together with those remarkable books that are perhaps her finest, part memoir-narrative, part lyric essay. Recognizing the "magic distortion"[1] inherent in works of the imagination, she declared that her work was "a quite skillful arrangement of fact and fiction."[2]

Gabrielle-Sidonie Colette was born in 1873 in the Burgundian village of Saint-Sauveur-en-Puisaye. Examining her childhood from the vantage point of maturity, she remarked that she could discern in her early years no intimations of an impending literary vocation. It is true that as a child she had been surrounded by books. Minet-Chéri, as her mother called her, or Bel-Gazou, the name her father preferred—a Provençal name meaning, prophetically, "speaker of beautiful words"—was an avid reader. At the age of seven or eight she plunged into the turbulent, often darkly-hued world of Balzac with a passionate interest that deepened through the years. Decades later she called the great nineteenth-century novelist "my cradle, my forest, my voyage."[3]

When she was in her teens, she sometimes talked about literature with her father, Captain Colette, a rather dashing meridional who, in 1859 at the age of thirty, had lost a leg in battle during the Italian campaign of Napoleon III. Forced to abandon a military career that had begun brilliantly, he had accepted the modest post of tax-collector in Saint-Sauveur. There he had met and married the widow Sidonie Robineau who, thanks to her first husband, was endowed with a small fortune and two small children. (In light of documents not yet completely published, it has been suggested that Captain Colette rather than Jules Robineau was the father of Sidonie's second child, Achilles, Colette's favorite brother.)[4] Sido, as Captain Colette called his wife, had two more children, of whom Gabrielle-Sidonie was the second. The deep love between Sido and her somewhat quixotic husband, whose life when measured by social standards might be deemed a failure, forms the foundation on which Colette later erects the subjective and highly stylized world of her childhood.

To keep abreast of the political, artistic and scientific events that were taking place in the world

from which he no doubt felt himself exiled, Captain
Colette subscribed to various journals which lay in
neat piles on his desk along with pens, blotters, seal-
ing wax and all the other paraphernalia of a writer's
trade. For, although Colette would not learn of it
until after her father's death in 1905, Captain Colette
nurtured the dream of becoming a writer. After her
husband's death, Sido found on one of the top shelves
in the study a dozen or so beautifully bound manuscript volumes, each containing a hundred or more
pages of fine paper. On the outside of the volumes,
Captain Colette had written titles. The pages themselves were blank except for a dedication on the first
page: "To my dear soul, her faithful husband, Jules-
Joseph Colette." "An imaginary work," writes Colette
of her father's abortive attempt to be an author; "the
mirage of a literary career."[5]

Despite the presence of a father, of siblings and
of books throughout her childhood, Colette's early
years, at least as she reconstructs them, were marked
most profoundly by her awareness of nature and by
her mother, "the principal figure of my whole life."[6]
The antennae of young Colette's sensitive and alert
spirit were keenly attuned to the natural world—the
garden, the countryside and the plants and animals
that shared them with her. Over this world presided
Sido, a matriarchal deity whose knowledge of plants
and animals was inexhaustible, the goddess Gaea,
residing at the center of all things. "Sido and my
childhood, one and the other, one because of the
other, were happy at the center of an imaginary star
whose eight points had the names of the cardinal and
collateral points of the compass."[7]

As the above sentence suggests, Colette's portrayal of her childhood is no mere recollection, more

or less objective, of past days. It has a visionary quality, a mythical dimension. For her, childhood is a "lost
paradise," a homeland she had abandoned and which,
by her own admission, she was then unworthy of
regaining. Everything associated with her early life is
bathed in the luminous light of a paradisiacal vision.
Even her grammar school is "a kind of rough and
tumble paradise" enlivened by a bevy of "disheveled
angels."[8] Returning time and time again to her childhood and to the image of Sido, the "pure spring"[9]
from which she never ceased to drink, Colette elabo-
rates, slowly and for over half a century, a personal
version of the Garden of Eden. There she had once
lived, "a young girl, intransigent, beautiful, absurd."[10]
The lyricism that flows broadly and serenely through
Colette's work reaches its finest expression in those
pages that evoke her childhood and nature. In such
pages, and there are many of them in her work, Colette's prose acquires the resonance of poetry, whose
function it is, she once declared, to make us "forget
reality, to promise the world marvels, to sing victories
and to deny death."[11]

The particular reality that Colette often wished
to forget but that haunted her imagination for years
was her marriage to Willy and her awakening to
sexual love. In the figure of Willy she clearly saw the
jinn who not only led her from the garden of paradise into the murky world of Parisian society, but who
also enticed her—a willing victim, she admits—from
the world of girlhood innocence into the world of
sexual pleasure. The garden of paradise–Parisian society; girlhood innocence–sexual pleasure; plants and
animals–human beings; joy–sorrow. This list of pairs
could be extended. In each, the first element has a
positive value, the second, a negative value, or at least

an ambivalent quality. In each, the two elements are
contradictory, complementary and in dialectical relationship to each other. Furthermore, all such pairs
may be subsumed in the master pair Sido–Willy, a
duality as central to Colette's world as Eros and
Thanatos, the life and death instincts, are to Freud's.

The words "Sido" and "Willy" have then a considerably broader meaning than the simple referential
meaning of Colette's mother or Colette's first husband. They are constitutive symbols, to borrow a term
the aesthetician and philosopher of literature Eliseo
Vivas used in his analysis of D. H. Lawrence,[12] and
have the function of suggesting the two fundamental
categories through which Colette grasps experience;
they are the two categories that give her world its
basic order.

In some respects Colette's work is curiously Mani-
chaean, for it records the long and arduous conflict
between the polarities of Sido and Willy. Colette even
tends to use different literary genres to express each of
these two categories: all the novels and virtually all
the short stories deal with love and the relationship
between men and women, which is nearly always
unhappy; they are written largely in dialogue that is
crisp, economical and thoroughly idiomatic; in her
meditative, essayistic works and in her descriptions of
nature, composed under the sign of Sido as surely as
the novels were conceived under the sign of Willy,
the sentences swell and arch spaciously, become
astonishing parabolas of sound and rhythm, buoyed
up by a lyricism that is usually suppressed in the
novels.

Who then was Willy? Much has been written
about him, and yet we know very little about his
character. Son of a distinguished Parisian publisher,

gregarious, ebullient, a complicated man whose conversation was full of wit, ostentatious erudition and
obscenities, his real name was Henry Gauthier-Vil-
lars. Among the many pseudonyms he used, "Willy"
was to become the most famous. Writing twenty-five
years after her divorce, Colette readily admits that
she never really knew him, and adds that nobody else
did either.

She had fallen in love with him in 1890 or 1891
when she was about seventeen. To most of Colette's
acquaintances and to Colette herself he no doubt
seemed to be an unexpectedly good match. (After
the break-up of the marriage, Colette insisted that
Sido had never approved of Willy.) He may even
have appeared to be something of a godsend, for
Colette's family was now virtually penniless. Captain
Colette had failed to nurture Sido's fortune (tied up
mostly in real estate) with the care that such matters
demand. Debts had slowly accrued; finally, in 1890
the family had been forced to leave their house and
auction off their belongings. Having nowhere else to
go, they moved in with Achilles, the oldest son, who
had married and was now a country doctor in the
neighboring village of Châtillon-Coligny. It was there
that Colette met Willy, whose father Captain Colette
had known years before in the army. Clearly, Willy
came along at an opportune time.

Fifteen years her senior, bald, bearded and cor-
pulent, Willy (or Monsieur Willy as Colette always
wrote of him in her books) was a familiar figure in
the journalistic circles of Paris, where he was well
known for his gossip columns, serious articles on scientific and historical matters, and music criticism.
Indeed, he was an ardent Wagnerite and did much to
promote the German master's music in France during

the 1890s. Having a genuine taste for what was good in the musical avant-garde, he also defended the music of Debussy, César Franck, Fauré and D'Indy, helping to turn public opinion in their favor. Above all, however, Willy was known for his fluffy, mildly risqué novels that had in fact been ghostwritten. An habitué of the demimonde, an entrepreneur whose interest in literature was strictly commercial, Willy, who had a mania for having himself (and later his wife) photographed, was an early and brilliant manipulator of public opinion by means of skillful publicity and adroit advertising.

That Colette loved him deeply there is little doubt. Years later in *Mes Apprentissages*, 1936 (*My Apprenticeship*), a book which, despite its title, is not devoted to a discussion of literary or artistic matters, but to a recounting of her relationship with the formidable Willy, Colette casts a cruel, implacable light on a love she feels was betrayed. Deliberately debasing her former love for Willy, she attributes it to the "burning sexual impetuousness that throws too many impatient little beauties into the clutches of seducers half consumed by age."[13] Indeed, throughout *Mes Apprentissages* there runs a furious rage against sexuality as well as a willful attempt to exorcise it. Writing about her early relationship with Willy, Colette uses a vocabulary that abounds in somber words: fear, victimized child, prey, disgust. Her love for Willy was, she declares flatly, nothing but an ugly adolescent fantasy:

Being young and ignorant, I was at first intoxicated—a guilty kind of intoxication, an adolescent impulse, frightful and impure. There are many girls of scarcely marriageable age who dream of being the showpiece, the plaything, the dissolute masterpiece of an older man. It is an ugly desire which they do penance for by getting what they wanted, a desire which is associated with the neuroses of puberty, the habit of nibbling on chalk and coal, of drinking mouthwash, of reading dirty books and of sticking pins into the palm of one's hand.[14]

In Colette's literary world, and this is the underlying theme of all her major novels, "the exhausting sexual pastime,"[15] which is usually called love but which is in fact as different from love as impurity is from purity, is an imperious physical need that can be fulfilled only in sorrow and at the expense of a distressing loss of independence. It might be objected that this is a limited and unsatisfactory view of the relationship between men and women. Of course it is, and Colette's work illustrates, relentlessly in novel after novel, that no satisfactory relationship between the sexes can be established on the basis of such a premise. However, it is pointless to criticize Colette for her concept of love. Perhaps only a countrygirl who has married a Willy may adequately judge how truthfully love is depicted in Colette's novels.

After her marriage in 1893, a new life began for Colette—a life which, as far as we can judge, she had anticipated optimistically but which soon became embittered. Colette discovered, as many, perhaps most girls do, that marriage, which had seemed so interesting and desirable before the wedding, was not the unmitigated joy she had expected. In fact, it was a bitter pill. In *Noces*, 1943 (Marriage) she describes her wedding fifty years earlier; she concludes with the remark that "the next day a thousand leagues, chasms, discoveries, irremediable metamorphoses separated me from the day before."[16] As she left with Willy to catch the train to Paris, her "heart swollen with grief," she saw Sido "standing in the little kitchen in front of the blue-tiled stove, her face marked by an expression of terrible sadness, pensively preparing the morning chocolate."[17]

Recalling her wedding day, Colette uses two significant images to describe herself: "a dove stabbed to the heart," and "a wounded bird." They are indicative of the emotional tone associated with love in all her novels. Love in Colette's world entails the loss of a peculiar kind of poetry, composed, as she herself defines it, of solitude and independence.[18] That a woman loses solitude and independence when she gets married is indisputable. Equally undeniable is the fact that Colette's concept of love and marriage is more familiar to women than to men. In fact, Colette's work, as it evolves throughout five decades, reflecting both the author's inner landscape and the world around her, conforms to the three-stage archetypal pattern of a woman's life—virgin, wife and matron. As a chronicle of a woman's destiny, it is surely one of the richest and best sustained in literature.

But the revelations of her wedding night and the loss of independence do not alone account for Colette's deep suspicion of love. Her work reflects something more than that universal human attitude toward love which Catullus summed up in his famous phrase, *Odi et amo* ("I hate and I love"). It has its orgin in an event that occurred about a year after her marriage.

Willy had at first installed his bride in his bachelor apartment, filthy, drafty and strewn with dirty German postcards celebrating underclothes and buttocks. Soon they had moved to a small, third-floor apartment in the rue Jacob, which was cleaner but still sunless and cramped. Willy seemed to know everybody in Paris. He trotted his young wife around to all the first nights, concerts and receptions, exhibiting her at all the fashionable events and smart cafés that were an integral part of the life of a certain segment of Parisan society during *La Belle Époque.* Despite the social whirl, or perhaps because of it, Colette felt desperately lonely. Willy, who was expanding his literary factory, hiring young but penniless writers to churn out spicy, saleable novels which he then published as his own work, was much too busy with his sundry activities and numerous mistresses to devote much attention to his wife or to help her adjust to her new life.

Then, several months after her marriage Colette received an anonymous letter informing her of Willy's infidelities with Charlotte Kinceler, a poor but spunky girl from Montmartre whose language was full of lower-class slang that vastly amused Willy and his literary friends. Colette went to the place of rendezvous and, indeed, found them together. In *Mes Apprentissages* she insists that this scene effected a final rupture between the past, now the locus of happiness, and the present, irremediably associated with suffering. Characteristically, she expresses this idea in pairs of words that belong unmistakably to the constitutive symbols of Sido and Willy:

Before the Kinceler incident awakened in me the feeling of danger, the taste for survival and for self-protection, I had great difficulty in accepting the fact that there is such a difference between the state of an unmarried girl and the state of a wife, between country life and life in Paris, between the presence (or at least the illusion) of happiness and its absence, between love and the laborious, exhausting sexual pastime.[19]

The words "taste for survival" ("le goût de durer") are important. Colette sees in the refusal to give up, in the will to persist, one of the most common of feminine traits; virtually all the heroines in her novels possess it. It was a trait that she now discovered in herself. After "the Kinceler incident," Colette's principal concern was to hide her unhappiness from Sido. For thirteen years she was to play the comedy of marital happiness before Sido's alert and penetrating gaze. At first, the emotional strain seemed too great, and Colette fell so desperately ill that her doctor despaired of saving her. Sido rushed to Paris and spent weeks nursing Minet-Chéri back to health.

Colette's convalescence was long and, as convalescences tend to be, monotonous. To distract his wife, Willy suggested that she write a journal about her schoolgirl days. Wishing to refresh her memory and no doubt eager to return to the country, Colette persuaded Willy to take her to Saint-Sauveur so that she could see once again her old school. In July 1895, they arrived in Saint-Sauveur, causing considerable excitement among the schoolgirls who boarded in and had not yet gone away for the summer. Colette and Willy dined in the school refectory and spent the night in one of the private rooms next to the dormitory. A few years later Colette gave a fictionalized account of this visit in *Claudine en ménage* (1902). They then went on to Bayreuth where they attended the Wagner festival. She later used Bayreuth as the setting for several scenes in *Claudine s'en va* (1903).

Back in Paris, Colette dutifully set about performing the task Willy had assigned her: she was to write her girlhood memoirs. She purchased a notebook of the kind she had used in school, and, sitting down at her desk, began to write industriously but with the lack of interest that often characterizes students who are hurrying to finish some bit of tiresome homework. When she had finished, she handed the manuscript to Willy. He glanced at it and then put it in a desk drawer, saying it was worthless. "I returned," wrote Colette, "to my sofa, my cat, my books, my new friends."[20]

Two years later, while clearing out his desk, Willy found the manuscript, reread it, and decided that if a little spice were added it might sell. Colette set to work again, touching up the text here and there according to Willy's specifications. Entitled *Claudine à l'école* (*Claudine at School*), the book was published in 1900 under Willy's name. Carefully organizing a publicity campaign, Willy saw to it that a picture of a girl adorned the book's cover. In the preface he coyly hinted that a girl had in fact collaborated with him, divulging secrets of a particularly piquant nature.

"And that," explains Colette, "is how I became a writer."[21]

2

Claudine

C *laudine à l'école* is the first of five novels tracing the girlhood and married life of Claudine who, if not identical with Colette, nevertheless incarnates certain important facets of the author's experience. It is presented as a journal written by the fifteen-year-old heroine who recounts the events of her last year in school. The body of the book consists of some two hundred pages of improbable and often amusing episodes, followed by fifty pages devoted to a finely articulated description of the final examinations; this in turn is topped off with an account of a raucous country dance, which ends the novel.

The book begins with a sentence that is artfully naïve, suggesting, as it does, Claudine's youth and innocence while also pointing coyly to the probability of changes to come: "My name is Claudine, I live in Montigny; I was born here in 1884; I shall probably not die here."[1] After a brief description of the village of Montigny, Claudine launches into a two-page celebration of the "beloved woods" that adorn the countryside. These two pages are interesting for a number of reasons. Their lyricism is in sharp contrast to the rest of the novel which is essentially a series of schoolroom incidents, dominated by dialogue and strung along on the most tenuous of plot lines. Both the lyrical style and the taut, economical style that together characterize Colette's work are present then in her first book.

The opening pages reveal other features that are characteristic of Colette's work. Nature, for example, is clearly contrasted to society. Claudine likes to be alone in the woods. The presence of other girls, foolishly afraid of snakes, spiders and briars, prevents her from enjoying the delicious solitude and independence that are associated with the forest. In opposition

16

to this well-ordered world of beautiful and harmless creatures, is the school, a closed, turbulent world of adolescent girls who are boisterous, deceitful, ingenuous, preoccupied with forbidden things and supervised by adults who are by and large a tatty lot. The polarity between nature and society—a polarity which Colette establishes in the first pages of *Claudine à l'école*—will be sustained throughout her entire work.

It is significant that in her description of the forest Colette does not depict trees as living things that push upward and conquer a perpendicular segment of space. Her description does not evoke in the reader's mind notions such as elevation or upward movement. Depriving trees of verticality, Colette endows them with horizontality. They "ripple and wave over there in the distance as far as the eye can see."[2] Our eyes are not directed upward, but either toward the horizon, as in the above sentence, or more frequently to the ground. Claudine never looks up at the sky nor glances at the leaves that are presumably above her. No birds fly through the air; indeed, there is virtually no air, no open space, in this world. (In fact, very few birds inhabit Colette's animal kingdom. One of her later heroines, Renée Néré in *La Vagabonde*, recalls "the deep, thick forest without birds"[3] that formed part of the décor of her childhood. Renée, a writer, even wrote a novel entitled *The Forest Without Birds*). Whereas in much of world literature and painting trees create a sense of upward motion, in Colette's world they have no such ascensional power.

This lack of verticality reveals a fundamental characteristic of Colette's literary world, for it is a world which has no immediately discernible ascensional dimension, or, to express it metaphysically, no obvious transcendental dimension. It appears to be earthbound. If birds are by and large absent from Colette's world, so are the sky and clouds; nor do mountains constitute a significant feature of her land-scape, although she traveled extensively in France and frequently saw the Alps. Working later as a jour-nalist, she wrote more than one article in which she gave her impressions of riding in a balloon. The arti-cles are curiously lacking in any sense of eleva-tion. Colette describes what she sees below her as if she were walking in a garden looking at the flowers at her feet. It is surely no accident that most of the action in her fiction takes place in rooms that are closed and often small.

Excluding the notion of verticality from her description, Colette devotes her attention to the forest floor which is covered with little flowers and small creatures. The woods themselves are depicted as an intimate world full of protective nooks and hidden sanctuaries. The words "little" and "narrow" reappear constantly, as well as images of objects that are enclosed or curled up on themselves. The valleys are "so narrow that some of them are ravines"; a snake is "rolled up in a spiral"; paths are narrow. When it rains, Claudine huddles up under an oak tree where, well protected, she listens to the rain beat on the forest's "roof." There is a pond, "smooth and deep, surrounded on all sides by the woods"; in the middle of the pond there is a little island. The ravines, too, are "deep," and the woods themselves are "deep and thick." The adjectives "little" and "deep" combine to create a sense of intimacy with and penetration into nature. Claudine shivers deliciously as she walks through the woods, startled by little scurryings and rustlings, by strange noises and unexpected sights. But there is no real danger here; "he wasn't dangerous," she says of the little snake. On the contrary, Claudine's intense pleasure and her participation in the processes of nature underscore the fact that she is at home in the woods which are for her a kind of refuge.

In her mature works, Colette will seldom write descriptions so obviously rooted in her own psychic need for an asylum, a retreat. The descriptive passages in her mature books will be more visually vibrant, more sensually perceptive and less ornate. But for Colette, nature will always represent a refuge from the world of society and the hypocrisy of men.

The dozen or so characters in the novel are a colorful lot, although they are essentially two-dimensional. In lieu of a real plot, the story hangs together first by virtue of a clearly delineated time sequence, marked by the change of seasons and by the approaching examinations at the end of the school year; secondly, the reader feels a certain forward movement or progression which results from the description of emotional relationships that form, break up and re-form with different partners.

At the beginning of the novel, Claudine has a short-lived crush on Mlle Aimée, the young, languid and self-centered assistant mistress who was born, so it seems, to be a kept woman. The vivacious Claudine sets out to tame (*apprivoiser*) Mlle Aimée. The word *apprivoiser* is important in this context. It is the word normally used for the domestication of animals and suggests the dialectic of domination and subjugation. The first sketchy depiction of love in Colette's fiction (here sororal affection might be a better term, although as usual in the Claudine books, relationships are deliberately ambiguous) is presented in terms of conquest and enslavement, a dual concept that will tend to characterize love in all of Colette's novels.

Colette's view of love as a frustrating encounter between two partners whose needs are essentially different and who never succeed in communicating with each other—a view enunciated in the first of the Claudine books—is no doubt a reflection of her relationship with Willy. It may also be, perhaps only tangentially, a reflection of the economic and social status of women at the turn of the century. The Marxist critic Claude Roy has suggested that by viewing love as a kind of submission to a superior force Colette has accurately represented the situation of women in a capitalistic society;[4] for, according to Marx, such a society subjugates women to men and men to money.

Roy, to say nothing of Marx, may have overstated his argument, but certainly if one looks at the legal status of women in France around 1900, it is no exaggeration to say that, juridically at least, women were dominated by men. Until 1893, for example, the year of Colette's marriage, a woman doing the same work as a man received half his pay; furthermore, what she did earn went to her husband, for it was not until 1907 that women were granted the right to control their own money.[5] It is not unlikely that such a state of affairs deepened Colette's feeling that the relationship between men and women, certainly between Willy and herself, was one of jailer and prisoner ("man, the lovable jailer," she once wrote).

In *Claudine à l'école* Colette considers love from yet another point of view. Claudine's cat, in heat once again, looks at her mistress and seems to plead: "Don't despise me too much; nature makes imperative demands. But I'll come back soon and I'll lick myself a long time to purify myself of this shameless way of life."[6] Sexual instinct is here presented as an irrepressible force of nature that demands satisfaction even though it can be gratified only in impurity. Sexuality, which is usually the principal ingredient of love in Colette's fiction, is a kind of daemon that forces its victim to abdicate his independence and even to desire his own sorrowful enslavement.

Although religious concerns are completely foreign to Colette, whose world has no God save perhaps nature itself (the Archbishop of Paris refused to permit Colette's body to be buried according to the rites of the Church), there is something curiously Augustinian about her perception of a world which harbors a force that is both tyrannical and impure. Indeed, she devotes a whole book to the subject of purity and impurity, entitling it *Le Pur et l'impur*, 1932 (*The Pure and the Impure*).

Since Colette is so often portrayed as a kind of natural creature who lived according to and in harmony with her instincts, it is important to realize that there runs through her work a nostalgia for an impossibly pure nature, unsullied by the particular demands her cat referred to. This yearning for purity, this wish to lick herself clean, finds its ultimate expression in the books of her mature years, written at a time when she seems to have come close to rejoining Sido in a realm untroubled by sexuality. Not that Colette was unaware of the danger implicit in aspiring to a purity that is ultimately unattainable, that is in fact contrary to nature. Indeed, she analyzes the inhuman and unnatural quality of purity in two of her best novels, *Chéri*, 1920, and *La Chatte*, 1933 (*The Cat*). But whereas in these two novels, as well as in others that figure among Colette's best books, the pure and the

impure are presented in terms of a struggle that has
a tragic dimension, in the Claudine books they are
simply ingredients in a potpourri of titillating anecdotes.

Claudine à l'école is full of sly innuendos, knowing smirks, kisses in dark corners and cloakroom gossip about the goings-on in the bushes. Claudine's brief
infatuation with the assistant mistress at the beginning
of the novel is soon expanded into a genuinely Lesbian
affair between Mlle Aimée and Mlle Sergent, the ugly
red-headed headmistress. Male instructors from the
adjacent boys' school hover around Claudine and her
classmates, sizing up their charms. The town doctor,
reputed to be Mlle Sergent's lover, visits the school
rather too often, and, after patting the girls paternally
on the head, lets his hands stray a bit. For readers
whose tastes are more eccentric, Colette throws in a
mildly sado-masochistic relationship between Claudine
and the new girl, little Luce. As is usually the case in
libertine novels, there is a lot of peeking behind doors.
Couples are often discovered in compromising situations; the most notable example is in the final scene
when, during the clamorous annual dance held in the
school house, the headmistress is found in bed with
the doctor.

Although Claudine à l'école has few pages free
from self-conscious winks and schoolgirl snickers, it
also has genuinely funny scenes told in a language
that bubbles and sparkles with irresistible glee. In spite
of an occasional tendency to overwrite and to depend
too heavily on exclamations, Colette has a firm control
of language even in her first novel.

Nevertheless, Claudine à l'école is not a distinguished work. Devoid of intellectual substance, it was
designed primarily to titillate. It will not do, I think,

to blame Willy alone or even primarily for the coy
dalliance with vice in this and later novels. Titillation
is woven so tightly into the very fabric of *Claudine
à l'école*, a novel which is essentially the portrayal of
a world simultaneously—or at least alternately—innocent and perverse that I am inclined to see in it one
of the modes Colette used to express her persistent
concern with the pure and the impure. In short, titillation resulting from an artful toying with debauchery
is one of the veins Colette worked, and it crops up
even in the books of her maturity.[7]

Claudine makes it plain that although she joy-
ously participates in the world of her school and
indeed shares most of the preoccupations of her classmates she is really different from and superior to
them. "I have never had schoolmates of my own
kind,"[8] she says, explaining that the other bourgeois
families in the village send their children away to
school while only the daughters of peasant families
attend her "fantastic school."[9] If her mother were still
alive (Colette never portrayed her own mother in her
work, not even indirectly, until after Sido's death in
1912), she too would no doubt be sent away to school.
But her quirky, likeable father, an absent-minded
malacologist who spends most of his time writing a
book on snails and slugs, lets his tom-boyish and high-
spirited daughter do as she pleases. Surrounded by
people of questionable probity and honesty, Claudine
is more intelligent and somehow purer than those
around her; she maintains her own integrity without
becoming in any way self-righteous. This particular
kind of solitude, composed of integrity and superiority
to circumstances, characterizes most of Colette's fictional heroines, as it does Colette herself.

Other themes that are developed in Colette's

later novels are also adumbrated in *Claudine à
l'école*: jealousy, of course, although here it is treated
lightly and only in passing; an intense desire for independence ("Anything that is at all like imprisonment
makes me rabid,"[10] says Claudine) together with a
yearning for love which, alas, in Colette's world is
incompatible with independence. Thinking of the
gawky boys she knows, Claudine realizes that she
could never love any of them. The man she could love
would be "someone stronger and more intelligent than
I, someone who would bruise me a little, whom I
would obey."[11] Ardently, she wishes for the presence
of someone but does not know who he is—someone
"whom I shall love and know fully" (no doubt an
oblique comment on Willy's unknowability). Claudine
realizes, as do all of Colette's heroines, that to wish for
such a thing is to ask for the impossible, for in
Colette's world no real communication between
human beings is possible. Wisely but sadly she dis-
misses the matter from her mind with the remark that
it is just another pipe dream.

Colette herself was later severe in her judgment
of the Claudine books. "All the Claudines play una-
bashedly at being little girls, silly girls,"[12] she wrote.
She reproached herself for having composed cruel
caricatures of people she had known in Saint-Sauveur
and for being totally indifferent to the effects that the
book would have on the lives of the individuals concerned. The headmistress at Colette's school, who in
no way resembled the vicious, Lesbian tart of the
novel, was particularly hurt, and Colette came to
regret the irresponsibility she had shown in creating
the fictional Mlle Sergent.

But she also suggests other reasons for her dislike
of the Claudine books. She deplored her readiness to

perform whatever was demanded of her—Willy of
course did the demanding—and the ease with which
she obeyed. Colette never forgave herself for signing
over the sole rights of the Claudine books to Willy.
Although the books were a prodigious commercial success, Colette never received a penny from them.
(Willy rashly sold the rights around 1910, thus letting
the goose that laid the golden eggs get away from
him.) Significantly, Colette's dislike of the Claudine
books extends to a condemnation of virtually all the
art and literature of the period:

French art has already been through deplorable periods in
which everything, even literature, seems to suffer under a
kind of humiliating curse. There can be no redemption for
the products of a tiresome age that festooned itself with
taeniae. A retrospective show of 1900 would arouse only
horror, except for some of the feminine fashions, graceful,
long-veiled and angel-like.[13]

The art style that Colette here condemns is what
the French in 1900, using the English words, called
"modern style," and what the English, using the French
words, called "art nouveau." The French words were
later accepted by art historians, and Art Nouveau is
the term now used to designate a particular style that
flourished briefly but intensely in art, fashion, interior
design and architecture around 1900, then died
around 1905 only to be partially revived, especially
by fabric designers, in the late 1960s.

Jean Cocteau and others have suggested that Colette's art has certain affinities with that of impression-
ist painters. It is certainly true that both Colette,
particularly in her descriptive passages, and the
impressionists were concerned essentially with physicality, with the sensuous quality of matter and the

texture of things. But Colette's art also has, I believe, affinities with Art Nouveau. Indeed, two important aspects of Art Nouveau are part of Colette's own aesthetic: (1) a particular way of portraying women and (2) a distinctive style in the depiction of nature.

The women of Art Nouveau paintings (there are very few men in these paintings) are curiously hermaphroditic. The frigid, androgynous beauty of their faces often expresses a smoldering sensuality. In his discussion of Art Nouveau, art historian Peter Selz has called attention to the sexual ambivalence of the females that stare, coldly and yet suggestively, out of the paintings and drawings of Art Nouveau artists. They are, in Selz' words, "descended from the hot-house creature of the Pre-Raphaelites and have the ambivalent eroticism of a small-breasted, narrow-shouldered, virginal, indeed often boyish creature."[14] The heroines of Colette's early fiction—the tomboyish Claudine with her tiny breasts, Rézi who is Claudine's Lesbian friend in *Claudine en ménage*, Annie in *La Retraite sentimentale*, Minne in *L'Ingénue libertine*, as well as other shadowy figures of the demimonde— all have the peculiar ambivalent eroticism of the women in Art Nouveau paintings.

In her handling of nature, too, Colette reveals certain affinities with Art Nouveau. Using fluid, melodious, undulating lines, Art Nouveau artists created sinuous shapes, climbing stalks, clinging tendrils. They often depicted plants and especially flowers in minute and accurate detail. Indeed, many of them were careful students of botany. The long flowing hair of the women in their paintings often merges with plants and becomes part of a general wavy configuration, leaving no more air or space in the composition than does Colette in the description that opens *Claudine à l'école.* Essentially an ornamental art, Art Nouveau slipped often into preciosity and affectation, an accusation that has been leveled more than once at Colette.

In some of her most amusing pages, Colette describes the interiors of fashionable Parisian homes in 1900. She readily admits that she shared her contemporaries' taste for curvilinear motifs and for eccentricity. Indeed, all her life she continued to like the undulating line, surrounding herself with objects that were round and convoluted. She abhorred angular shapes and maintained that circular, sinuous shapes rest the eyes and quiet the mind. (Perhaps her love for cats was derived in part from her passion for the arched and wavy form.) For years she collected antique paper weights, eventually acquiring a collection that became famous. In the speech she delivered in 1936 at her reception into the Belgian Royal Academy, Colette spoke of her "instinctive fondness for curves, spheres and circles."[15] Her love of curves is reflected in the shape and rhythm of her language. Virtually all her descriptions of nature (and nature for Colette as for Art Nouveau artists is usually a garden) have as their most prominent feature long, convoluted sentences that twist and wind, unfolding their meaning in a rhythm that is slow and beautifully paced.

Colette's harsh judgment of Art Nouveau is part of her blanket condemnation of the *fin-de-siècle* society to which Willy had introduced her. In his *Journal*, André Gide notes that he, too, brushed against this society, "artificial, sophisticated, hideous."[16] Adding, with the outrageous self-righteousness which sometimes marks his *Journal*, that "an unconscious residue of puritanism" protected him from this milieu, Gide remarks that Colette, "despite all her superiority," seems to have been somewhat contaminated by it.

Gide's comment is perceptive. For, although Colette looked back to the beginning of her literary career with a certain displeasure and even a touch of bitterness, the whole corpus of her work, especially her fiction, which is full of aging courtesans, gigolos and other curious human fauna that flourished in the demimonde of *La Belle Époque*, bears stigmata that betray the year 1900.

Claudine à l'école was an immediate bestseller. Capitalizing on the book's popularity, firms began making Claudine dresses and Claudine hats; shops sold a Claudine lotion, a Claudine perfume, a Claudine ice cream, Claudine cigarettes. Willy, billing himself as the father of Claudine, was seen everywhere, usually accompanied by his wife who, many contemporary observers noted, had large eyes and a funny little fox-like face. The next few years were grand ones for Willy. By 1904 he was so famous that actor Sacha Guitry wrote of him: "I know only God and perhaps Alfred Dreyfus who are as well known."[17] A few months after the publication of the first Claudine book, Willy and Colette moved out of the modest apartment in the rue Jacob and, after a brief stay in an artist's studio, settled down in a fashionable mansion; their neighbor was Prince Bibesco.

Eager to take advantage of the public's infatuation with Claudine, Willy soon got his wife back in harness and instructed her to write another Claudine novel. To make sure that she would not dawdle, he locked her in her room four hours a day, assigning her a certain number of pages to write. Colette did not really object. Having no literary ambition for herself, she seems to have been rather amused by the whole affair. Moreover, she soon discovered that she could deliver the goods as well as any of Willy's other ghostwriters. From 1900 to 1905 she wrote one book a year, all of which were published under Willy's name.

Claudine à Paris, 1901 (*Claudine in Paris*) is presented as a continuation of Claudine's journal. Now seventeen years old, Claudine has moved to Paris where she lives with her father in an apartment in the rue Jacob. She explains that, distressed at leaving her woods, "which are what I love most in the world,"[18] she fell ill; now that she is recovering, she has decided to take up her journal again. At Willy's suggestion, Colette liberally sprinkled patois and girlish argot throughout the novel. Addressing herself to an audience that devoured huge quantities of libertine novels, she increased the dosage of titillation and filled the book with exclamations and double entendres. The result is a style that is often disagreeably coy and at times intolerably mannered.

Loosely constructed, the novel is composed of brief scenes showing Claudine as she moves into a society that is relatively fashionable and mildly perverse. Few pages of the novel are free from allusions, often coyly oblique, to sex. Even Claudine's cat contributes once again to the provocative tone, for early in the novel she goes into heat. The servant, who has the curious habit of walking around the apartment, her breasts cupped in her hands, scours the neighborhood to find a tom that will satisfy the poor thing, adding that it is time for Claudine, too, to find herself a lover. Sexual inversion, a theme that was present in *Claudine à l'école*, figures even more prominently in *Claudine à Paris*. Homosexuality is in fact a theme that reappears in Colette's early books with the persistence of a nervous tick. The boyish Claudine meets

her effeminate cousin Marcel who, although he is only
seventeen, seems to be as experienced in pederasty
as Proust's Charlus.

In *Mes Apprentissages* Colette explains why she
created Marcel. Willy, Colette says, was rather jealous
of her and managed to isolate her from people her
own age. Men between the ages of, say, twenty and
thirty-five were kept at a safe distance, except for the
hacks who were in Willy's employ and pretty much
under his thumb. To compensate for the lack of
attractive male acquaintances, she created the young
man Marcel; by portraying him as a homosexual, she
made him harmless in her own eyes and thus freed
herself from the inhibitions she may have had about
describing a male who was young, handsome and
charming. Perhaps; however, creatures of an ambivalent sex continue to populate much of her work long
after Willy has disappeared from her life. "The seduc-
tion which emanates from a person of uncertain or
dissimulated sex is powerful,"[19] declared Colette in
1932.

Although Colette created many beings of an
uncertain sex, she seldom, if ever, created viable adult
male characters. Her males are either older men
(Willy figures, observed from a distance as in the
Claudine books), young men who are singularly imma-
ture, as in *Le Blé en herbe* and *Chéri*, or sketchy,
shallow figures, usually feckless husbands or lovers,
mere pawns, as in *Mitsou, Duo* and a number of
other novels.

Whatever function Marcel may have had for Colette herself, in *Claudine à Paris* he has the function of
precipitating a number of crises and of intensifying
the atmosphere of piquancy. Passionately fond of con-
fidential revelations, he urges Claudine to describe

her school days in Montigny and her relationship with
little Luce; he, in turn, reveals his love for a certain
Charlie. Luce herself turns up in Paris where she is
now the mistress of her sexagenarian uncle, whose
eccentric tastes include pursuing his mistress around
the room on all fours.

In the midst of all this roguish activity, Claudine
remains too determinedly bright-eyed to be convinc-
ing as a character. In the end, the seventeen-year-old
heroine falls in love with Uncle Renaud, Marcel's
handsome and urbane father, who is forty years old.
There is little doubt that the seductive and paternal
Renaud embodies certain aspects of Willy. Another
side of Willy's complex character is represented by
the music critic Henry Maugis, who crops up in
Claudine à Paris as well as in several of the novels
that were ghostwritten by other of Willy's hacks. Colette affirms that she did not write these passages, and
that Willy, infatuated with his own image, created a
caricature of himself in the figure of Maugis and then
slipped "Maugis scenes" into various of the novels
that were published under his name.

Maugis is shown only in animated conversation.
He is not so much a fictional character as a kind of
excuse for a torrent of puns, obscenity and arcane
erudition. Colette mentions that when she wrote the
fourth Claudine book, *Claudine s'en va*, Willy told
her to leave a few pages blank and he would write
in some Maugis scenes. Procrastinating as usual when
it came to writing, for although he knew exactly what
he wanted out of his ghostwriters he was apparently
quite unable to face the task of writing it down himself, Willy did not manage to get the necessary pages
written. Colette tried her hand at pastiche and, find-

ing that she had a knack for it, wrote all the Maugis
scenes herself in *Claudine s'en va.*

Two other features of *Claudine à Paris* are
worthy of note. Claudine meets Marcel and Renaud
while paying a visit to her aunt, who has lived in
Paris for years. In her description of Aunt Coeur's
apartment, Colette stresses certain details that, by dint
of subtle insistence, acquire peculiar significance
within the economy of the passage, creating a particular mood and suggesting the character of the inhabi-
tant. In her major novels, descriptive details are never
gratuitous. As Colette acquired greater confidence in
her skill as a writer, she pared down and cut out. Her
mature art is economical and sparse, often a prodigy
of understatement. Every detail of scenery and décor,
every allusion to the quality of light in a room or to
the tone of a person's voice is strategically placed.
Together, such details create a uniform tonality con-
sistent with and indicative of the particular human
drama that is taking place. Novels such as *Chéri, Le
Blé en herbe, La Chatte* and *Duo* are slender but
skillfully contrived artistic pieces, each with a distinctive tone or atmosphere that is cunningly sustained
from beginning to end.

Aunt Coeur, who resembles Empress Eugénie,
lives in an apartment that is fashionably decorated in
white. Electric lights and sparkling crystal objects
intensify the atmosphere of relentless modernity and
implacable brightness. The apartment is in perfect
harmony with the world in which Aunt Coeur moves
—the artificial and often heartless world of the Parisian salon. Only in her bedroom, which is not visible
to the guests who stream through her salon, does
Aunt Coeur drop her social mask and reveal another
aspect of her nature: all the furniture, now hopelessly

out of fashion, that had been in her room when she was a girl, is carefully preserved in her bedroom, evoking the happy days of girlhood. The polarity of Sido and Willy is illustrated in even as peripheral a character as Aunt Coeur.

As Claudine falls in love, the dilemma of independence and submission, central to Colette's analysis of love, is introduced, although it is treated only fleetingly. "My freedom weighs heavily upon me, my independence wears me out," muses Claudine before understanding that the key to the mystery is her growing love for Renaud: "What I have been seeking for months without realizing it—for even longer—is a master. Free women are not really women."[20] With such thoughts buzzing through her head, Claudine accepts Renaud's offer of marriage, and the novel ends on a note of fairy-tale romance.

The year 1902 saw not only the publication of Colette's third novel, but also the highly successful stage adaptation of the first two Claudine books. Willy had discovered a young Algerian music-hall performer, had christened her Polaire, trained her for the role of Claudine, directed her in the play, and then witnessed her enormous success, which marked in fact the beginning of Polaire's career as a dramatic actress.

Polaire somewhat resembled Colette, although Colette's waist was considerably bigger than Polaire's famous eighteen-inch waist. Willy decided that as a publicity stunt he would dress the two women alike and parade them around in public, a double incarnation of Claudine. Since Claudine, during her illness at the beginning of *Claudine à Paris*, had been obliged to have her hair cut, Colette, much to the dismay of Sido, cut off her own long hair, instigating a revolution in feminine hair styles. With short hair and dresses shorter than the then prevailing fashion, Polaire and Colette prefigured the bobbed hair, tomboyish type of woman that was to become a familiar figure in the 1920s.

Claudine en ménage (translated into English first as *The Indulgent Husband* and then later as *Claudine Married*) is by far the best constructed of the Claudine books. Continuing her journal fifteen months after her marriage, Claudine enunciates the subject of the book in the first sentence: "Definitely, there is something wrong with our married life."[21] Starting with the premise that there is a mysterious flaw in her marriage, and indeed in the very nature of marriage, Claudine recalls the highlights of the last fifteen months, and then, in the latter part of the book, moves on to an account of her brief but intense Lesbian affair with the beautiful Rézi.

Claudine's vague dissatisfaction with married life—a dissatisfaction that has nothing to do with a lack of love, for Claudine and Renaud love each other—stems essentially from two sources, both of which have their origin in Colette's own life and go a long way in explaining the emotional dilemmas of her fictional heroines. Before her marriage, Claudine had hoped to find in Renaud a master who would dominate not only her body but her mind and spirit as well; she had hoped to find in her husband an infallible authority to whom she could joyfully submit, a kind of divine will whose categorical dictates would give form and meaning to her life: "I ardently hoped that Renaud's will would bend mine, that his firmness would master my rebelliousness, that ultimately he would have the strength that his eyes seemed to promise, accustomed as they were to commanding and captivating."[22] In sum, she sought a lover who would also be a kind of father-God figure.

Renaud, as Claudine sadly discovers, qualifies admirably well as a lover but fails miserably as a figure of authority. Like many of Colette's male characters who seem to devote their lives exclusively to the pursuit of sensual pleasure, Renaud has numerous moral and even physical characteristics that Colette defines as feminine, a word which, in her vocabulary, is generally synonymous with weak. (In one of her last books, Colette casts an unsympathetic glance at most of the men in her fiction and judges them in a neat phrase: "Devoting oneself to sensual pleasure is not a career for a respectable man."[23]) Renaud's shoulders and upper arms have a kind of feminine plumpness; there is something coquettish about the way he holds his chin, and indeed about his whole person. Decidedly, Claudine concludes, "Renaud is more of a woman than I am."[24]

Indeed, if there is something feminine in Renaud's makeup, there is definitely something masculine or strong in Claudine's. It would be a grave mistake to see in this nothing but the sly toying with inversion that too often marked *Claudine à l'école* and *Claudine à Paris*. In *Claudine en ménage* Colette's presentation of the character differences between Claudine and Renaud touches on a personal problem that Colette discusses further in *Le Pur et l'impur*, a book which deals with a broad range of problems related to sexuality.

In a section of this book presented as a conversation between herself and the actress Marguerite Moreno, one of her oldest and truest friends, Colette discusses the "genuine mental hermaphroditism which burdens certain people who are of a very complex nature." "So many men," notes Moreno, "have a feminine quality in their character."[25] To make sure that her comment is not interpreted as a reference to pederasty, she adds: "I repeat: in their charcter." Realizing that both she and Colette have a masculine streak in their character, she asks: "Why can't you resign yourself to the fact that certain women represent for certain men a danger of homosexuality?" By describing certain traits in Claudine's character as masculine (and Colette often equates masculinity with intellectual vigor, moral superiority and even a certain asceticism), Colette has suggested the difficult situation of a superior woman married to or in love with an inferior man. This situation, rarely treated in literature despite its commonplaceness in life, was no doubt Colette's own and is a persistent theme in her fiction.

The second reason for Claudine's dissatisfaction is her gradual realization that she and Renaud are separated from each other by an insuperable barrier that is itself the inevitable consequence of their love. Throughout her work, Colette insists on the fundamental difference between a woman's experience of sensuality and that of a man. Sex, for her, is not a meeting, a joining, a union in elemental Oneness; rather it is irrefutable proof that such a union is illusory; it is an affirmation of solitude: "One could say," writes Claudine, "that for him—and I feel that this is what separates us—sexual pleasure is composed of desire, perversity, lighthearted curiosity and persistent eroticism. Pleasure for him is joyous, gentle and facile, whereas it crushes me and plunges me into a mysterious despair that I desire and yet fear."[26]

In *Le Pur et l'impur* Colette pursues further her

analysis of feminine sexuality; an aging Don Juan discloses the reasons for his deep-seated rancor against his many mistresses:

By what right did they always get more out of it than I? If only I could suspect that they didn't! But I had only to look at them. Their pleasure was only too genuine. Their tears, too. But above all, their pleasure . . . To be their master in that pleasure, but never their equal—that is what I cannot forgive them.[27]

Recognizing the male's limited orgasmic capacity, Don Juan cannot forgive women for possessing greater sexual capacity than he, for surpassing the male in sexual insatiability. In another of her books, Colette, contrasting male and female sexuality, notes: "A man's sensuality is but a brief season."[28] When Colette writes that "a woman knows that she is just about inexhaustible," or that "man is less made for woman than woman is made for man,"[29] she is expressing an insight into the nature of female sexuality that is perhaps debatable but that to her seems self-evident.[30]

Feeling that her present life is vaguely unsatisfactory, Claudine asks Renaud to take her back to Montigny for a brief visit which turns out to be, as she says, "an adieu to my young past." Their visit to Claudine's school gives Colette an excuse for reverting to the formula of provocative anecdotes that had contributed to the commercial success of *Claudine à l'école*.

Back in Paris, Claudine meets Rézi, the beautiful wife of a retired English colonel. To convey Rézi's mysterious but powerful charm, Colette, a lover of the undulating line, resorts to images of curves and graceful arches:

I immediately saw one of the principal origins of her charm: all her movements, the undulation of her hips, the curving of her neck, the rapid raising of her arm to her hair, the swaying of her seated body, formed curves so much like circles that I could see the design of interlacing rings, of the perfect spirals of sea shells that her gentle movements left outlined in the air.[31]

Lesbian love had been treated in nineteenth-century novels by authors as distinguished as Gautier (*Mademoiselle de Maupin*) and Balzac (*La Fille aux yeux d'or*), to mention only two. Like pederasty, it was a standard feature of the libertine novels that multiplied around the turn of the century. Colette had of course broached the subject in her first two books but had treated it only triflingly. There is little doubt that Rézi was introduced in *Claudine en ménage* to sustain the interest of those readers who had come to expect a dose of inversion in the Claudine books. However, Colette gave them something considerably different from what they had been accustomed to; instead of treating the subject exclusively *à la libertine*, she analyzes the motives of a Lesbian relationship, writing, in the classical tradition, a kind of *roman d'analyse*. Claudine turns to Rézi only after analyzing the malaise she associates with her marriage. When she realizes that Rézi loves her, she exults: "The joy of being loved, of hearing it said to me, the joy of a miser who has lost something precious and found it again, the victorious pride of feeling that I am something more than an exciting toy."[32]

Claudine's words recall Colette's own confession that before her marriage she wished to be the licentious plaything of a mature man. Like Claudine, Colette now wished to be "something more." Indeed, about the time she was writing *Claudine en ménage*, she began to feel her way, tentatively and cautiously at first, toward greater independence from Willy. She had convinced her husband that she could write faster away from the distractions of Paris. Always eager to increase his revenue, Willy bought a country house, Les Monts-Boucons, in Franche-Comté, where Colette could live alone for some six months out of the year, churning out the goods and sending them posthaste to Willy's Parisian publisher. When Willy was particularly engrossed in one of his more absorbing amatory intrigues, he even asked his wife to vacate their Parisian apartment for a time and to retire to the country. Off Colette went, taking with her a pen and plenty of paper.

As well as suggesting Colette's growing desire to break away from Willy, *Claudine en ménage* reflects another aspect of Colette's private life. Willy, whose contacts were extensive in Parisian society, had introduced his wife into certain homosexual groups, one of which was feminine. It was dominated by the Marquise de Belboeuf (known to her friends as Mitzy or Missy), who was separated from her husband and who dabbled in the theater, writing skits and pantomimes as well as acting on occasion. In 1903, Colette was even induced to act in an amateur production of one of Missy's pantomimes. Increasingly interested in the theater, Colette began to take dancing lessons. Although she could not have known it at the time, she was starting to prepare herself at about the age of thirty for a career on which she would have to depend for her livelihood after her separation and divorce from the redoubtable Willy.

The way in which Colette made her first contact with the Lesbian world is no doubt reflected in *Claudine en ménage* and surely helps explain the curious

role played by Renaud, who actively encourages the
relationship between his wife and Rézi. Prompted by
a kind of perverse gaiety, he rents a *pied-à-terre* in
which the two women can meet undisturbed by Rézi's
suspicious husband; refusing to give them the key,
the debauched Renaud escorts them cheerfully to
their tryst. The liaison between the two women comes
to an abrupt end when Claudine discovers Rézi in
bed with Renaud. Breaking off all contact with Rézi,
Claudine regrets that Renaud had not been strong
enough to protect her from her own masculine desire
to dominate the seductive Rézi. He had been indulgent when he should have been commanding. Once
again the dilemma of masculine dominance and
feminine submission ("a perhaps fallacious vocation
of servant,"[33] is the way Colette expresses it elsewhere) emerges as the underlying theme of the novel.

Encouraged by an unprincipled husband, Claudine strayed onto the shores of Lesbos and, despite her
initial favorable impression, found the island inhospi-
table. Hurt by the betrayal of Rézi and Renaud,
Claudine, like a wounded animal, flees; she goes
back to Montigny. But the return to Montigny is
more than a simple return to a precise geographical
spot; it is a return into self, a disengagement from the
external world. "Where is the home I can go back to?"
asks Claudine. "Within myself. Dig into my suffering,
into my irrational and indescribable suffering, and
lie down curled up in that hole."[34]

That Colette herself eventually took this road
back into self is certain. That she, like Claudine,
moved briefly and temporarily in Lesbian circles is
also indisputable. If either circumstances or Colette's
nature compelled her to reside for a brief time in
Gomorrah (a city which Proust, she says, completely

misrepresented in his great novel), the fact remains that once freed from the rotund incubus that was Willy, Colette created no other major fictional heroines who dally with Lesbianism. Whenever the subject is again mentioned in her work, it is with a note of sadness and compassion, as in the following passage which in fact enriches the meaning of Claudine's relationship with Rézi, purifies it of the monotonous libertine tone that permeates the Claudine books, and puts it in a perspective doubtlessly closer to Colette's own view on the matter:

Two women enlaced will never be for him [a man] anything but a depraved couple, and not the melancholic and touching image of two weak beings who have perhaps taken refuge in each other's arms, to sleep, to weep, to flee from man who is often cruel, and to taste, better than any pleasure, the bitter happiness of feeling that they are alike, small, forgotten.[35]

The weakness of *Claudine s'en va*, 1903 (literally, Claudine Goes Away; translated first as *The Innocent Wife* and later as *Claudine and Annie*) is mainly the result of its imperfect focus. It tries to be two things at once and falls between two stools. Still, it is of considerable autobiographical interest, showing as it does a heroine who leaves her husband; it anticipates Colette's separation from Willy by three years. Claudine, reunited with Renaud, recedes into the background and becomes one of the secondary characters. The heroine this time is Annie and it is *her* journal, not Claudine's, that we are reading.

At the beginning of the novel, Annie represents one ideal of womanhood—an ideal usually held by men. Even as a girl of twelve she was completely devoted to Alain. Their marriage was a foregone con-

clusion. As Alain's wife, she continued to be totally
dependent on her husband who arranged every
detail of her life, even deciding which dresses she
should wear. Alain, insufferably pompous and self-
centered, congratulates his wife on being "so attached
to her husband and to her pretty house which is clean
and tidy."[36] When he goes to Buenos Aires to settle
an inheritance, he leaves Annie alone with a list of
instructions about what she is to do and what she is
not to do, whom she may see and whom she may not
see.

Frequenting a society that includes her vulgar
sister-in-law Marthe—who locks her novelist husband
up for three or four hours a day so he will write
(Colette here fantasizes vengefully)—Maugis, the
sententious music critic who becomes Marthe's lover,
and Claudine, whose vocabulary is now racier than it
was before, Annie begins to break out of the chrysalis in which she has for so long been imprisoned.
Her gradual awakening, her realization that life in
Alain's shadow is a pseudo-life, is the basic theme of
the book and one that is potentially of great psychological and dramatic interest. However, it tends to
get lost in the incessant conversational patter that
makes up the surface texture of the book. First in
Paris, then at a fashionable French spa, and later at
Bayreuth, Annie's friends keep on talking tirelessly.
Some of the conversation is quite funny, particularly
the satirical comments that are prompted by the
stodgy atmosphere of that musical Mecca, Bayreuth.
But much of it soon palls, and the hapless reader is
left with the distinct impression that he has spent an
hour or two listening to a conversation that is vacuous
and silly.

Little by little Annie frees herself from the

oppressive image of Alain. Her discovery of a packet
of love letters proving that Alain had a mistress liber-
ates her completely from the husband she no longer
loves. "A slavish creature, unconscious of its chains—
that is what he has made of me,"[37] Annie declares.
From now on she is going to be responsible for her
own life.

In the long conversation with Claudine that ends
the book, Claudine advises her to get a divorce. Not
that a divorce will be easy. In 1903 a divorce left an
irradicable smudge on a woman's character, which
moreover partly explains Colette's reluctance to leave
Willy. Claudine, like Colette, was also well aware of
the crushing loneliness that may be a divorcée's lot.
"You will see a number of unpleasant people who will
shuffle papers," Claudine warns her; "then there will
be the divorce, all the blame placed on Annie—and
freedom." To which Annie, like an existential hero
who is overwhelmed by the burden of freedom,
replies anxiously: "Freedom. Is it a very heavy burden,
Claudine? Is it terribly difficult to manage? Or rather
will it be a great joy, the cage door open, the whole
world before me?"[38] Claudine, of course, cannot
answer. Annie must find out for herself, which is the
subject of the last Claudine novel, *La Retraite sentimentale*. "To choose one's own suffering," muses
Annie; "some people would make of that an ideal of
happiness."[39]

Another aspect of *Claudine s'en va* deserves to
be mentioned. Although Claudine advises Annie to
divorce Alain, she herself did not divorce Renaud. On
the contrary, she and Renaud are now completely
reconciled. Renaud's character is not consistently portrayed from one book to the next (Colette later said

he was as hollow and empty as a Christmas tree decoration).[40] The Renaud of *Claudine s'en va* is not the repellent rake he was in the preceding book. Indeed, Claudine and Renaud are so totally engrossed in their love that the external world has virtually ceased to touch them. At the end of the novel, just as Annie prepares to leave for an extended trip, eager to throw herself into the hustle and bustle of life, Claudine suddenly announces that she too is leaving; but unlike Annie, who is rushing toward the world, she plans to withdraw from it: "I'm not staying, Annie. I've already gone. Can't you feel that? I've left everything . . . except Renaud . . . for Renaud. Friends are traitors, books are deceivers. Paris will see no more of Claudine. She will grow old among her relatives, the trees, and with her lover and friend."[41]

On the surface, this intention to trot off to the country and, like an older Paul and Virginie, live a life of bliss among the beloved trees may seem absurdly sentimental. But as Claudine begins to slip out of Colette's fictional world, yielding the spotlight to other heroines, she takes with her a primordial vision of happiness that never ceased to haunt Colette. Nearly all of Colette's novels recount the loss of love and the resultant solitude (*Gigi*, more of a fairy tale than a novel, might be considered an exception; however, it ends before Gigi and Gaston are married; the trouble, Colette well knew, begins only *after* the marriage). Annie and Claudine are at a crossroad. Annie's path leads toward a world defined by the constitutive symbol of Willy; Claudine's toward that represented by Sido. Colette's art as well as her life is characterized by an alternation between these two categories of being.

By 1904 Colette felt the need to write something other than potboilers for Willy. Turning to the world of animals, she wrote four dialogues in which the two interlocutors are Toby-Chien, a male bulldog, and Kiki-la-Doucette, an angora cat who, despite his feminine-sounding name, is also a male. Lurking in the background, but seen only through the eyes of the two animals, are He and She, the owners. The slender volume was published in 1904 under the title of *Dialogues de bêtes* (Animal Dialogues) and was the first book to bear Colette's name, Colette Willy. The dedication read: "To amuse Willy." The following year three more dialogues were added as well as a laudatory preface by Francis Jammes, and the book was reprinted with the title of *Sept Dialogues de bêtes* (Seven Animal Dialogues). It was later enlarged once again, and now appears in the definitive edition of Colette's work as *Douze Dialogues de bêtes* (Twelve Animal Dialogues).

As a child Colette had been surrounded by animals, for Sido was always taking in stray cats and dogs. In 1903 Colette told a reporter representing the periodical *La Vie Heureuse* (*Happy Life*): "I have only one dream: to live in the country where, in the solitude of the mountains, I can gather around me as many domestic animals as possible."[42] At Les Monts-Boucons she had ample opportunity to realize her dream, and did indeed surround herself with animals. Even in her first books, animals, particularly the cat, played a significant role; they would continue to populate her fictional world. As well as introducing animals in her fiction, and even making a cat the principal character of one of her most successful novels, *La Chatte*, Colette devoted a number of books, often collections of articles written for special occasions or for newspapers, to descriptions of animals, usually animals she had lived with.

Indeed, Colette does not discuss animals abstractly. Each has a distinct character. It is true that in *Dialogues de bêtes* Toby-Chien and Kiki-la-Doucette speak undeniably with the voice of Colette; however, in her later animal books, particularly *La Paix chez les bêtes*, 1916 (Peace Among Animals, included in an English edition entitled *Creatures Great and Small*), and *Paradis terrestres*, 1932 (Terrestrial Paradises), Colette tries to divest her writing of some of the anthropomorphism that inevitably creeps into books on animals; she strives to view animals as beings who have an autonomous existence outside the human world rather than as creatures whose only raison d'être is to perform certain functions in the world of man.

Much, too much I believe, has been written about Colette's presumably uncanny rapport with animals. The public, which often feels compelled to create legends around famous people, eventually fashioned the legend of a Colette who possessed the primitive and fabled talent of communicating with beasts. Photographed countless times with dogs and especially cats, Colette rather cultivated this image of herself. She certainly did nothing to modify the public's notion that she was a feline spirit encased in a woman's body.

Her love of animals was not of the sentimental kind. She respected their integrity, their nonhumanness, and treated them with patience. She also had a strong will which usually compelled animals to obey her. "I like to have the last word with children and animals,"[43] she wrote late in life. To call Colette, as D'Annunzio did, "my sister in Saint Francis of

Assisi,"[44] is to coin a pretty phrase but to miss the
mark completely. It is not Colette's rapport with animals that is remarkable; the astonishing thing is that
many of her early readers were apparently so iso-
lated from the animal world, so insensitive to non-
human forms of life, that they found in Colette's
instinctive bond with nature something marvelous,
strange and incomprehensible.

For Colette, the chief difference between animals
and humans is that animals are innocent whereas
humans are not. Animals are governed by instinct
which Colette defines as innocence, while humans
pervert their instinctual urges with reason, the source
of duplicity and hypocrisy. Instinct, which is of course
outside the moral categories of good and evil, may
induce an animal to kill, as Colette illustrates in the
pages devoted to her pet tiger Bâ-Tou.[45] But it will
not lead an animal into vice or depravity, for these
are peculiarly human attributes. The animals in Colette's books thus belong to the world of innocence
and purity that is represented by the constitutive symbol of Sido. Like the garden of childhood, they are
an integral part of the peaceable kingdom which is
Colette's vision of lost happiness.

The slight preciosity of the language in *Dialogues
de bêtes* contributes, I believe, to the charm of the
conversation between Toby-Chien and Kiki-la-Doucette, although it must be admitted that some readers,
notably the critic Ernest Charles who read the book
when it first came out, have found these little sketches
intolerably pretentious. Certain themes emerge from
the urbane banter of the two genteel animals who,
although dependent on their owners, also lead animal
lives in which their masters play no part.

In the pages she devotes to animals, Colette deals

repeatedly with the ambiguities of a relationship that is characterized by dependence as well as independence. Toby-Chien and Kiki-la-Doucette are both humble and gentle. Colette's world will soon be populated with humble creatures. Her strenuous years in the music hall will teach her to admire the modest, uncomplaining girls who, by dint of hard work and often with only a modicum of talent, manage to make their own way in a world that is usually hostile and callous. Unlike Balzac's characters who, as Baudelaire observed, are all geniuses (even the janitors), Colette's characters possess no special gifts. They are modest and unassuming, generally unheroic, indeed often distressingly mediocre. Unremarkable as they are, Colette treats them with unfailing sympathy and understanding.

As well as being the first book Colette published under her own name, *Dialogues de bêtes* is also the first book in which she consciously aimed at creating a literary style. The section entitled "Le Premier Feu" ("The First Fire") is a kind of duo in which Toby-Chien and Kiki-la-Doucette alternately address fervent rhapsodies to the fire that has been lighted in the fireplace. That their language is marked by a deliberate striving for the artful expression, the telling word, is not surprising. Much of the literature of the period—that of Pierre Louÿs and Marcel Schwob (one of Colette's few friends in the 1890s and a writer who no doubt contributed significantly to the formation of her literary tastes) as well as the early works of Gide —reveals the same tendency. Although Colette later condemned "prose of this type, devoid of simplicity and even of clarity, with phrases full of twists and arabesques and the interplay of syllables,"[46] it left its mark on her own prose style, as it did on Proust's.

Along with her attempt to forge a literary style, Colette wished to experiment in literary genres and to try her hand at third-person narrative. She wrote a fifty-page novella, a "conte fantastique" as she called it, which she entitled *Minne* and intended to publish under her own name. It was, she says, a little study in red, rose, black and pale gold. Willy saw the story's potential and obliged his wife to expand it into a novel which was published under his name in 1904. At Willy's urging, she wrote a sequel, *Les Egarements de Minne* (Minne's Aberrations), which was published the following year, again under Willy's name. Somehow Colette managed to keep the rights for herself, and in 1909 she touched up the two little novels and published them together as a single novel under the title of *L'Ingénue libertine* (*The Gentle Libertine*). The manuscript of the original fifty-page novella was never published and has been lost.

In the preface which she wrote in 1949 to the definitive edition of *L'Ingénue libertine*, Colette expressed reservations about the book's literary worth. Although it is indeed a slight work whose two parts are quite independent of each other, it has a certain charm, especially the first part. The fifteen-year-old Minne, as delicate, pale and golden-haired as an Art Nouveau heroine, fantasizes in her rose-tinted bedroom about Apaches who, with red scarves and blood-stained knives, roam through the streets at night. She longs to be the girlfriend of their leader, a certain Le Frisé (Curly), and to "obey him passionately." One night she goes looking for her ideal lover, does not of course find him, and returns home, exhausted. Although the heroine is rather too silly to sustain a narrative of much length, the little story is told with a grace and gentle irony that turn it into a kind of fable.

Clearly, in *Dialogues de bêtes* and in *Minne* Colette was cautiously trying to find her own way and to
get off the treadmill she had been on, much to Willy's
benefit, for the previous five or six years.

3

The Vagabond

By 1906 Colette and Willy had been married for more than twelve years. Why had she stayed with him so long? Colette herself was later intrigued by that question and tried to answer it in the last chapter of *Mes Apprentissages*. As might be expected, she can give no simple answer. "It never occurred to me to run away," she states. "Where could I go? What could I live on?"[1] Too proud to return to Sido and admit that her marriage had been a failure, she was also terrified by the prospect of having to fend for herself. And so she hung on, devoting more and more time to dancing and acting.

Since her thick Burgundian accent, characterized by sonorously rolling r's (a trait she confers on several of her fictional heroines, including Claudine) would be, she thought, a distinct disadvantage in spoken roles, she decided to specialize in pantomime. Late in 1905 she began working seriously with the young and gifted professional mime Georges Wague, who afterward became her partner in many vaudeville routines. Colette's first professional performance as a mime took place on February 2, 1906, at the Théâtre des Mathurins. Willy handled the publicity, and when Colette, dressed as a faun, rushed on stage in pursuit of nymphs, the audience greeted her with enthusiasm. Although her talents as an actress were not particularly remarkable, she worked like a trouper and managed to project a stage presence that struck many spectators as extraordinary. When, a few months later, Willy suggested slyly that he might be able to arrange a long tour for her, perhaps even a tour abroad, Colette realized that she was being shown the door. "While I was dreaming of running away," she wrote with a touch of bitterness, "right next to me someone was planning conveniently to show me the door—my own door!"[2] Indeed, it was Willy who finally suggested that they separate.

By the summer of 1906 she and Willy had gone their separate ways, although they would not be divorced until 1910. Having no money of her own and unable to count on writing for an immediate income (the reading public knew her only as the author of the slender *Dialogues de bêtes*), Colette had, she says, few courses of action open to her: she could take to the streets or she could become a music-hall artist. She chose the latter career, although in the early 1900s a career in the music hall was considered scarcely less scandalous and immoral than that of a streetwalker. Shunned by many of her former acquaintances, she wrote a touching letter to Francis Jammes, the distinguished author who had graciously provided a preface for *Dialogues de bêtes*: she informed him that she was breaking off their correspondence to save him the embarrassment of writing to a music-hall artist.

For six years Colette, now in her middle and late thirties, danced her way around France, playing the vaudeville circuit. Some of her performances brought her a certain degree of notoriety. In 1906, shortly after her separation from Willy, she was engaged by Lugné-Poë, the celebrated director of the Théâtre de l'Oeuvre, for a small part in a play called *Paniska*. In the last act, Colette pranced on stage, almost naked, leading a procession of Dionysian revelers. The legend of a naughty Colette was to accompany her the rest of her life. Her most notorious performance, however, took place in January 1907 at the Moulin Rouge. In a skit called *Le Rêve d'Egypte* (The Egyptian Dream), Colette played opposite the Marquise de Belboeuf (Missy), who impersonated a man. A prolonged stage

kiss between Colette and Missy, whose Lesbian incli-
nations were known to many in the audience, caused
a scandal. Insults were hurled at the couple, objects
were thrown on stage, fighting broke out in the audience, and the curtain had to be brought down. The
Prefect of Police intervened, declaring that Colette's
partner in *Le Rêve d'Egypte* must henceforth be a
man. At subsequent performances Wague assumed the
role created by the excessively demonstrative Missy.

It was a hard life, characterized by daily re-
hearsals and performances, hours spent backstage in
drafty, dirty dressing rooms, constant travel and, perhaps most painful of all, an aching loneliness. It is
rather strange to think that Colette, who had a horror
of a certain kind of Bohemianism and who shared
with millions of other French bourgeois housewives
the passion for a tidy room and a well-arranged cup-
board, should have spent some six years in a milieu
which, to most Frenchmen of the time, was synonymous with immorality and Bohemian living. But the
very rigor of the life as well as the discipline required
to become proficient in a career she had adopted relatively late in life, served to protect her from the
seamier side of the music-hall business. Later she
always spoke of the music hall with gratitude; it was a
world in which "fantasy and bureaucracy were min-
gled. I can still evoke the dense limited element which
sustained me in my inexperience and fortunately
limited my vision and my cares for six long years."[3]

But the music hall did even more for her; it provided her with a legacy of experience which she
would soon transmute into fiction. *La Vagabonde*,
1911 (*The Vagabond*), *L'Envers du music-hall*, 1913
(*Music-Hall Sidelights*) and *Mitsou* (1919) all reveal
Colette's intimate knowledge of the music hall. In

fact, these three works, along with Toulouse-Lautrec's drawings and paintings of music-hall life, are probably the best portrayals we have of a now largely vanished form of entertainment.

Colette's music-hall career did not prevent her from writing. Thanks to Willy's practice of incarcerating his wife until she had written a specified number of pages, Colette had acquired the habit of writing regularly; she affirms that she even felt the need to write every day. The first work she published after her separation from Willy was, however, a continuation of her work as one of her husband's ghostwriters. In 1907 she published under the name of Colette Willy *La Retraite sentimentale* (The Sentimental Retreat), which is the last of the Claudine books and completes the years of Colette's literary apprenticeship. Begun at Les Monts-Boucons before her separation from Willy, the book, despite the usual dose of provocative situations, is in certain respects a novel of renunciation and new-found peace: "While I was writing *La Retraite sentimentale* . . . I was learning to live. Can you learn to live? Yes, if you are not happy. Felicity teaches you nothing. To endure without happiness and not to droop, not to pine, is a pursuit in itself, you might almost say a profession."[4]

In *La Retraite sentimentale* Claudine is once more writing her journal. She is living with Annie at the latter's country house, Casamène, a literary transposition of Les Monts-Boucons. Claudine's beloved Renaud is in a Swiss sanatorium from which he will return only to die. The book is composed essentially of two contrasting melodies: the low, grave melody of Claudine who knows instinctively that Renaud will not recover and whose quiet courage is sustained both by the intensity of her love for her husband and by a

kind of reabsorption into nature; and the high, strident
melody of Annie who, after leaving her husband,
became a nymphomaniac, traveled around Europe in
search of "fresh flesh," and now tells Claudine some
of her more notable adventures.

Annie's stories provide the main narrative content
of the book. To vary the scene slightly, Colette introduces Marcel, Renaud's homosexual son, who arrives
from Paris for an extended stay. Annie, ravenous after
a long period of abstinence, tries unsuccessfully to
seduce him. One of Annie's stories is of particular
autobiographical interest. She relates that she was
once pressed by friends to appear on stage as a mime.
After describing the makeup and costumes she wore,
she recounts her disastrous performance opposite "that
crazy mime, Willette Collie," whose passionate kiss on
stage one night caused such an uproar in the audience
that the curtain had to be lowered.

Annie is the last in a line of heroines that includes
Aimée, Luce, Rézi and Minne. All are ultra-feminine,
all possess to a superlative degree "the feminine
instinct of bowing down in worship,"[5] and all experience love only in terms of physical pleasure. Annie,
the last of this race, is the first to realize, or at least
the first to say, that sensuality is only one form of love,
only one aspect of happiness. "It's a very small part of
happiness," she tells Claudine, "but it's the part I have
chosen."[6] The heroine of Colette's next novel, *La
Vagabonde*, will also maintain that physical pleasure
is only a small part of love: "Sexual pleasure occupies,
in the limitless desert of love, an ardent and very
small place."[7] But neither Renée Néré, the vagabond,
nor any of Colette's subsequent heroines will choose
it as their lot; they will not, like Annie, deliberately

exclude from their vision of happiness other and more extensive forms of love.

Claudine's "moral isolation," as she puts it, her retreat into self, are reflections of Colette's mood during the years that followed her separation from Willy. Two themes are woven into the fabric of Claudine's meditations: the disintegration of her world and, concomitantly, the growing awareness that the crumbling of her world does not mean its loss, for it remains, pristine and intact, in the memory, whose function is precisely to conserve and embellish the past. Both themes are closely associated with the process of aging. Indeed, beginning with *La Retraite sentimentale* the notion of growing old becomes increasingly important in Colette's work. The beautifully serene works of her maturity have as their underlying theme "the supreme chic of knowing how to grow old" ("le chic suprême du savoir-décliner").[8] Few authors have charted as persistently and magisterially as she that segment of life's curve that moves from maturity back to the beginning.

The opening pages of *La Retraite sentimentale* set the introspective tone of Claudine's musings. Claudine examines her face in the mirror and notes "the first signs of disintegration."[9] The mirror image is particularly frequent in the works Colette wrote from about 1906 to 1912, the date of her second marriage, although it also appears in later novels. These were her music-hall days, and she often describes the care with which music-hall girls scrutinize their faces in a mirror as they put on their makeup. Approaching forty, Colette herself no doubt took extra care with her makeup, which is what Claudine decides to do when she notices the first telltale signs of age.

In Colette's novels, the examination of one's face

in a mirror usually leads to a bout of introspection, as
at the beginning of both *La Retraite sentimentale* and
La Vagabonde. But the mirror image has an even
richer meaning: it reflects Colette's growing consciousness of her function as an artist and her realization
that her work, despite all the deformations and trans-
formations inherent in the artistic process, is essentially a dialogue with self. At first she tries to detach
herself from Claudine. In *Les Vrilles de la vigne*, 1908
(The Vine's Tendrils) she declares her independence
from Claudine, a figure always too closely associated
with Willy to be completely congenial to Colette.
Turning away from the youthful Claudine, Colette
will soon begin to create a gallery of mature women,
the first of whom is Renée Néré, the most personal
and autobiographical of her heroines.

Signs of decay are visible, not only on Claudine's
face, but all around her. The garden is untended; the
wall is crumbling; "the pines are a hundred years old
and will not see another century, for the ivy is envel-
oping their trunks and strangling them."[10] Death is a
constant presence: the cat dies; Claudine's father and
Méline, the old servant, both die. The two seasons
that are described most frequently in *La Retraite sentimentale* are autumn and winter (winter scenes are
extremely rare in Colette's work). Renaud returns,
old and dying. There is a delicately plotted concord-
ance between Renaud's death and the gently falling
snow. Finally, and in muted tones, the novel concludes with a night scene:

It is getting dark. I have forgotten to have dinner, and
now the hour of sleep approaches. Come, my animals!
Come, little discreet creatures who have waited respect-
fully while I was dreaming. You are hungry. Come with
me toward the lamp which you find reassuring. We are

alone, forever. Come! We shall leave the door open so that
the night can enter with its scent of invisible gardenias,
and the bat who will hang on the muslin curtains, and the
humble toad who will crouch down under the door-step;
and so that he also can enter, he who does not leave me,
who keeps watch over the rest of my life and for whom I
close my eyes without sleeping in order to see him better.[11]

The notion that the past is vibrantly alive in the
memory is implicit throughout the entire novel. Like
Proust, two years her senior, but before him (for *Du
Côté de chez Swann* was not published until 1913),
Colette dwells on the subjective dimension of reality
and on that faculty of our mind which embellishes
what we love.

Claudine's retreat to Casamène is indicative of
Colette's first major retreat into that private corner of
self which Montaigne called the back room of one's
being—secret and impregnable. After 1912 or 1913,
Colette moved back out into the world, only to return
to the garden of childhood in a series of splendid
books published in the 1920s when she was in her
fifties.

The pieces that Colette collected and published
in 1908 under the title of *Les Vrilles de la vigne* were
first published in the weekly *La Vie Parisienne*. Short
sketches, some of which are narrative pieces but
many of which are essentially prose poems, they have
a certain unity of tone by virtue of the fact that they
were composed, by and large, at about the same
time and reflect the tenor of Colette's life at a particular moment. When she prepared the definitive edition
of her works for publication in 1949, she occasionally
moved pieces from one volume to another in order to
give each book a greater cohesiveness and inner logic.
Colette had a distinct preference for this type of

book, constructed of small, autonomous pieces which, when published together, complement each other and succeed in evoking a particular mood and in suggesting a particular nexus of ideas. *Les Vrilles de la vigne, L'Envers du music-hall, La Paix chez les bêtes, Les Heures longues, La Chambre éclairée, Le Voyage égoïste, Aventures quotidiennes, La Maison de Claudine* (which has nothing to do with the early Claudine novels), *Sido, Noces, De ma Fenêtre, L'Étoile Vesper, Le Fanal bleu,* as well as other works all belong to this category.

The famous title piece that opens *Les Vrilles de la vigne* is a fable: Once upon a time the nightingale sang during the day and, like other birds, slept at night. Then, one spring morning he awoke to discover that during the night tendrils from the vine on which he was perched had stealthily enveloped his legs, entrapping him. Terrified, he struggled. Only after an intense effort did he succeed in freeing himself from the tenacious tendrils. To avoid being entrapped a second time, the fearful bird vowed never to sleep during the season in which tendrils grow. And so, in springtime, the nightingale spends the night singing to keep himself awake.

After relating this little story, Colette identifies herself with the nightingale, concluding: "With a frightened start I broke all those twisted threads which were already grasping my flesh, and I fled. When the torpor of a new honeyed night weighed heavily on my eyelids, I remembered with fear the vine's tendrils and cried out in a lament, thus discovering my voice."[12] Colette here reveals the importance that writing has now assumed in her life. Quietly and in gently muted tones, she begins to sing. *Les Vrilles de la vigne* is in fact the first book that reveals the intensity of Colette's lyrical impulse—an impulse that finds its expression in prose poems of considerable stylistic virtuosity. Robust yet delicate, sensually vibrant yet exquisitely mannered, always beautifully modulated, Colette's prose in *Les Vrilles de la vigne* has a kind of Alexandrian refinement that may strike certain readers, especially those who seek social or political implications in the books they read, as excessively fastidious, somewhat like an eighteenth-century powdered wig. Later, Colette's prose loses some of its ornateness. In the novels of her maturity it tends to be lean and muscular. And in her last books, *L'Étoile Vesper* for example, the prose is grave and sober. It is still marked, however, by Colette's extraordinary sense of rhythm, which is no doubt the key to her style—one of the most distinctive prose styles in French literature.

As well as suggesting the crucial role of writing in her life, *Les Vrilles de la vigne* contains other themes, most of which are elegiac and tinted with melancholy. Figuring prominently among them is the theme of aging. Seated before her mirror, Colette muses: "It is my face of former days that I seek in this oval mirror I have picked up idly, and not my face of a woman, a woman still young whose youth is soon going to abandon her."[13] The desire to see herself as she once was is reflected in the many pages that evoke her childhood. One such sketch begins with the famous: "I belong to a land I have left."[14] Realizing that the country she left now has its reality only in her mind, she conjures up the features of that inner landscape: "the narrow valley," "the enchanted path that leads out of life," "the ancient forest where the world ends."[15]

The path Colette followed, however, was never

to lead out of life. She knew that human beings are
fallen creatures, that they no longer live in that state
of grace which she called purity and which, for her,
characterizes the world of children as well as the animal, vegetable and mineral kingdoms. Never a sentimental optimist, she viewed human life lucidly and
harshly. But she also knew that by watching intently
and humbly the plants and animals around her, and
by scrutinizing the reality of childhood which was
now preserved in her memory, she could restore a
form of innocence to her life. Indeed, an extraordinary
sense of purity emanates from Colette's work despite
the impurity of the human world she depicts. Her
own path now led to independence (and solitude),
to the music hall, and to writing. In a passage that
appeared in the first edition of *Les Vrilles de la
vigne* but was later shifted to *Dialogues de bêtes*,
Colette looks to the future:

I want to do what I wish. I want to act in pantomimes,
even comedies. I want to dance nude if my leotard bothers
me and spoils my figure; I want to go live on an island if
the whim should strike me, or associate with women who
use their charms to make their living, provided that they
are gay and light-hearted, even melancholic and wise, as
many such women are. I want to write books that are sad
and chaste, in which there will be only landscapes, flowers,
sorrow, pride, and the candor of charming animals who are
afraid of man. I want to cherish whoever loves me, to give
that person everything I have in the world: my body which
rebels against being shared, my so tender heart and my
freedom![16]

   With this list of wishes, we are already in the
world of Colette's next fictional heroine, Renée Néré,
the vagabond.

La Vagabonde, written backstage, in train sta-
tions and in cheap hotel rooms, was Colette's first
major novel, and it is by far the most intensely personal of her fictional works. The heroine, Renée Néré,
is a scarcely fictionalized portrayal of Colette herself.
The narrative core of the book—the account of
Renée's relationship with Maxime—is probably not a
direct literary transposition of a particular event in
Colette's life. However, it is close enough to events in
her life to allow Colette to elaborate on some of her
deepest concerns and, perhaps more importantly, to
give an artistic, and therefore gratifying, order to the
loneliness that was her lot in the years following the
breakup of her first marriage.

The novel is divided into three parts and is told
in the first person. Each part marks a crucial stage
in the relationship between Renée and Max, and each
has its own tonality and rhythm. As is nearly always
the case in Colette's major novels—which beginning
with *La Vagabonde* are all essentially psychological
novels composed within the terse, economical framework of the *roman d'analyse*—discreet references to
the weather and to seasonal changes in nature underscore the emotional state of the principal character or
characters. Part I covers the period from December
to, roughly, the end of January; Part II, from the first
of February to April 5; Part III, from April 5 to May
15.

Renée is a thirty-three-year-old divorcée who
earns her living as a music-hall mime. In the opening
scene, she is seated, painted and costumed, in her
small dressing room, waiting to go on stage for her
act. Images of solitude and of coldness are cunningly
and unobtrusively evoked in the opening pages of the
novel, setting the tone for all of Part I. Looking at

herself in the mirror, Renée is startled by her own
image which stares back at her. Detached and vaguely
disapproving, the figure in the mirror asks her: "Is
that you there, all alone? Why are you there?" ("Est-ce
toi qui est là, toute seule? Pourquoi es-tu là?")[17]

Like Valéry's *Jeune Parque*, who calls herself a
"captive vagabonde" and who in some ways curiously
resembles Colette's heroine, Renée begins to muse.
Both Valéry's famous poem and Colette's novel begin
at that moment in which consciousness is awakened
and startled into being. Surprised by her own image,
Renée is on the point of emerging from the state of
quasi-unconsciousness, of almost animal-like hiberna-
tion and inwardness in which she has been living for
several years. Perhaps even Renée Néré's curious
name, which rolls back on itself, repeating the same
letters in both first and last names, suggests the notions
of self-containment and introspection. It might be
pointed out that although the fictional Renée is based
essentially on Colette herself, she bears a faint resemblance to Colette's friend Renée Vivien, the Anglo-
American poetess who celebrated Lesbian love and
who died at the age of thirty-two in 1909, a few
months before Colette began writing *La Vagabonde*.

The numbing cold of a December day corresponds, of course, to a sense of numbness in Renée's
life. After the bitterness of her divorce, she had
emptied her life of any emotional attachment. She
withdrew from most of society and lived in a small
circle, symbolically represented by the tiny room
backstage, "this cage with its white wall," and by her
small, uncannily quiet apartment. The stage, too, is a
confined, delimited space; while performing, Renée
feels protected from the invisible audience by the

glare of the footlights and by the impersonality that results from the disciplined mastery of her art.

The fact that she is myopic and does not always clearly discern people and objects in front of her further emphasizes the distance between herself and the world around her. But suddenly, listening to the muted voice of her double in the mirror, she becomes conscious of both her independence and her loneliness. "Yes," she reflects, "this is the dangerous, lucid . hour."[18] The idea of waiting, which at first had seemed to be nothing more than part of the novel's narrative content, now assumes its full force. Not only is Renée waiting for the clock to read 11:10, the hour of her act; she is also waiting, fearfully and hopefully, for something to happen, for someone to tear open the protective chrysalis she has wrapped around herself. "Who will knock at the door of my dressing room, what face will place itself between me and the painted adviser who is watching me from the other side of the mirror? Chance, my friend and my master, will surely deign to send me once again the genies of his disorderly kingdom."[19]

After her act, Renée returns to her dressing room where she receives a note signed by the Marquis de Fontanges (Max): "Madame, I was in the first row of the orchestra; your talent as a mime leads me to believe that you possess other talents, more specialized and even more captivating; grant me the pleasure of dining with you this evening."[20] Chance has acted with remarkable precipitation. In four extraordinarily condensed pages, Colette has called forth her two protagonists; in bold, magisterial strokes she has arranged the stark confrontation between a man and a woman who now stand facing each other, as at the beginning of some solemn ritual.

The drama begins slowly and evolves in an atmosphere of "glacial fog." In Part I, Renée's past is evoked in a series of flashbacks, and her present life is described. Interspersed throughout the more introspective passages are vignettes of music-hall life, "a milieu in which nothing struck me as vile or bitter," wrote Colette in the 1949 preface to *La Vagabonde*. Each of Renée's three friends is, like herself, a kind of pariah: Margot was exploited by her husband and now lives alone with her dogs; the aging Hamond married a woman he adored, but his marriage turned out to be profoundly unhappy; Brague, the mime who is Renée's partner, lives solely for his art and has virtually no human contact.

With more than a touch of bitterness, Renée describes her marriage to the society painter, Adolphe Taillandy. Only after the publication of *Mes Apprentissages* did it become clear that Taillandy is Willy in virtually every respect. Indeed, even the names Taillandy and Willy are similar in sonority. Adolphe, a name of Germanic origin, may be an oblique reference to Willy's well-known passion for Wagner's music. In any case, Renée's grievances against her husband were precisely those of Colette against Willy.

Like Colette, Renée is a novelist as well as a mime. While married to Taillandy, she wrote and published three novels; all the rights, of course, were signed over to her husband. In two pages near the beginning of the novel, Renée rhapsodizes about the pleasures of writing and about her imperious need to "seize and fix . . . the iridescent, fugitive, bewitching adjective."[21] (The adjectival triad was as much favored by Colette as by Proust.) The voice here speaking is clearly Colette's. "There is nothing real," says Renée, "except dancing, light, freedom, music. There is nothing real except turning one's thought into rhythm and translating it into beautiful movements."[22]

In her list of what is real, Renée deliberately omits any reference to that old bugaboo, sex. Max, of course, with his crude, unsubtle invitation represents the danger of sex and the concomitant danger of a second entrapment in love. Although Renée rebuts his advances and has practically no contact with him throughout Part I of the novel, Max is always there. The reality he represents becomes the subject of Renée's (and Colette's) meditations:

Senses? Yes, I have them; I had them at the time Adolphe Taillandy deigned to be concerned with them. Timid, ordinary senses, content with the everyday caress which fully satisfied them, fearful of any refinement or licentious complications, slow to enflame but slow to extinguish, in short, healthy senses.

In a key passage she then explains the nature of her dilemma—a dilemma which, Colette intimates, is a fundamental feature of the feminine psyche:

Betrayal and prolonged suffering have anaesthetized my senses; but for how long? On happy days, filled with light-heartedness, I cry out: "Forever!" feeling myself pure, cut off from that which made me a woman like others. But there are also lucid days when I reason harshly with myself: "Be careful! Keep alert! All who approach you are suspect, but you have no worse enemy than yourself. Do not declare that you are dead, uninhabited, light as a feather; the beast you have forgotten is hibernating, and fortifying itself with a long sleep."[23]

Renée's problem was a central one for Colette as well as for a good many of her heroines. Being a woman means abandoning oneself to those sensual pleasures that can be procured only by submission to a master. Independence, or in Colette's telling phrase,

at least the "illusion of independence," and love are
mutually exclusive. For Renée, the conflict still
remains intellectual because she does not yet feel
attracted to her thirty-three-year-old admirer, Max,
whose persistent mooning she finds both tedious and
slightly ridiculous. At the end of Part I, however,
Hamond, who is a friend of both Max and Renée,
brings Max, uninvited of course, to Renée's apartment
for dinner. Gently, Max begins to insinuate himself
into her life.

Part II traces the path that leads from indiffer-
ence to love. The first pleasure Renée finds in Max's
company is that of satisfied vanity—"the vanity of
living in the presence of someone else."[24] Renée's
solitary life, which she had chosen as a kind of protective measure against love, now begins to seem
intolerably empty. When Max first takes her hand,
she is overcome by the need for companionship: "Oh,
to throw my arms round the neck of a creature, dog or
man, a creature who loves me"[25]—a cry which may
partly explain Colette's passionate interest in animals.
With Max's first kiss, Renée's dormant sensuality is
revived. "Female I was and female I find myself
again, for my pain and for my pleasure,"[26] she asserts.
But she does not give herself to Max. She knows, as
do all of Colette's major feminine characters, that sensual pleasure often leads to love, and that by accepting the former she runs the risk of finding herself
imprisoned in the latter.

In *La Retraite sentimentale* Annie had represented unrestricted sensual desire; she was contrasted
to Claudine who, after the death of Renaud—and
Colette may have disposed of poor, insipid Renaud in
order to establish the contrast—represents a love so
rarified, so devoid of physicality that it becomes an

adoration of an invisible presence. In creating Renée,
Colette molded a figure who is a combination of both
Annie and Claudine. More important, however, is the
fact that she used Renée to illustrate the profound
interrelatedness of sex and love in the feminine
psyche. When Colette, in a now famous sentence,
spoke of "those pleasures we lightly call physical,"[27]
she was referring to the process by which our physical
pleasures inevitably affect and in fact determine our
spiritual being. A man, Colette hints without elaborat-
ing on the subject, for the male psyche per se does
not interest her, may be able to separate sex and
love, physicality and spirituality. A mature woman like
Renée, however, cannot make this distinction; for her,
they form one continuous movement. If Renée calls
sexual desire the enemy within, it is only because by
yielding to it, she must inevitably yield to the enemy
without, that is, to man.

Renée's perception of man as an enemy is the
result of her marriage to Taillandy. Derisively she
defines marriage:

It is a question of conjugal domesticity, which turns so
many wives into a kind of nurse-maid for adults. Being
married is . . . how shall I explain it? It is trembling
because Monsieur's cutlet might be overcooked, his Vittel
water not cold enough, his shirt badly starched, his bath
water too hot! . . . It is: "Tie my necktie! . . . Cut my
toe-nails! . . ."[28]

The sardonic enumeration continues. Haunted by her
past, Renée is afraid of love. Even more, however, she
is afraid of having her love betrayed a second time.
Her age alone, she believes, would make such an
eventuality likely. But these fears tend to dissolve as
Renée feels the warmth of Max's growing love. Her

hesitation and her responsiveness are reflected in the
March weather, changeable and unpredictable. Colette's brief description of a stroll through the Bois de
Boulogne introduces a breath of air and a little sunshine into a novel from which they have thus far been
largely absent. Furthermore, the notion of physical
movement signals a quickening of the rhythm at the
end of Part II and is preparatory to the frenzied tour
of provincial theaters that Renée and Brague under-
take in Part III. Renée leaves in high spirits, eager to
return, for she has decided that after her return to
Paris she and Max will start a new life together.

It does not work out as she has planned. Part III
is an account of the tour, interspersed with Renée's
letters to Max. The letters are dated, which heightens
the effect of time's inexorable movement toward May
15, the date of Renée's return. The weather, which
was grey and rainy the day of her departure from
Paris, becomes warmer as she goes south. As the train
rumbles through the province in which she grew up,
Renée is plunged back into the paradise of childhood
which, she realizes, is beautiful precisely because it
is lost: "My country bewitches me with a sad and
fleeting enchantment every time I touch upon it, but
I would never dare to stop there. Perhaps it is beautiful only because I have lost it,"[29] she says, anticipat-
ing Proust's comment that the only true paradises are
those we have lost.

Although Renée and, indeed, the reader are quite
unaware of it at the time, Renée's confrontation with
her childhood dooms her dream of a happy life with
Max. The same psychological process that makes her
childhood beautiful because it is lost will prompt
Renée to preserve her love for Max by willfully sepa-
rating herself from him, thus ensconcing it, too, in the

past. Slowly, the reader senses, although he cannot be sure of it until the tension that mounts steadily through Part III is resolved at the end of the novel, that the tour itself is an image of Renée's flight from Max.

In the southern city of Avignon, Renée luxuriates in "the exuberant, the ephemeral, the irresistible spring of the Midi."[30] When Max, impatient and afraid of losing her, writes an urgent letter and proposes marriage, she is torn between her intense desire for him and her equally strong desire to remain independent. Marriage, which she views as "a sunny enclosure, bounded by solid walls," is sharply contrasted to her present mode of existence, "this easy, wandering life,"[31] characterized by loneliness and hard work, it is true, but also by a certain kind of autonomy. The thirty or so pages in which Colette lays bare Renée's heart are among the most penetrating she ever wrote. The subtlety of her psychological analysis and the beauty of her prose, whose complex harmonies and intricate rhythms make any translation a pale shadow of the original, are remarkable.

As Renée heads back north on the last leg of the tour, she leaves behind, in the sunshine of the Midi, the temptation of a happiness she dares not reach for because she is afraid of seeing it slip through her fingers. In discussing *La Retraite sentimentale*, I have called attention to the theme of disintegration; Claudine, watching her world slowly crumble, only to see it born again in her memory, is a reflection of Colette who, in the years just before and after 1906, witnessed the crumbling of her world. Renée represents a later stage in Colette's life. She bears witness to the fact that Colette has survived the collapse of her world and is now putting the pieces together, patiently and laboriously. But Renée is still too close to the event to be

anything but fearful; images of disintegration and of
loss float through her imagination, preventing her from
accepting the future with hope and confidence.
Renée's almost morbid concern with her age ("I watch
myself growing older with a resigned terror,"[32] she
says) is part of her lingering preoccupation with disintegration and with the end of things. In fact, the
novel concludes—fades out is a better word, for Colette ends it with three dots—on a softly falling
cadence as Renée, in beautifully tender tones, evokes
her own eventual death.

Given this preoccupation with a vanishing world,
one can understand the crucial function of art—both
writing and dancing—in Renée's (and Colette's) life.
In a sentence I have already quoted Renée affirms
that the pleasure of writing is in seizing and fixing
words, that is to say, in arranging them in an immuta-
ble order. In a world she perceives as unstable, she
satisfies her "need"—the word is hers—for order by
creating a new, artistic order of reality in her novels
and in her dancing. Max threatens the new order that
Renée has managed to impose upon her world; still
convalescing from marriage, she flees from the men-
ace he represents.

Returning home in the cold, gray dawn, Renée
writes her last letter to Max and dates it "May 15,
7 A.M." "I feel myself quite worn out, as though
unable to resume the habit of loving and afraid lest I
should have to suffer again because of it," she writes,
informing Max that she will not see him again. Seated,
as she was at the beginning of the novel, she looks
around the room:

It is a sunless morning and the cold of winter seems to
have taken refuge in this little sitting-room behind these

shutters that have been locked for forty days. Lying at my feet, my dog silently watches the door; she is waiting. She is waiting for someone who will never come here again.[33]

As Renée returns to the life she was living in December, images of coldness, solitude, smallness and waiting reappear. But there is a difference now. The grayness of her life is now tinged with "the red gleams of a heart-rending memory." "For a long time you will be one of the thirsts on my road,"[34] Renée cries out to a Max who is no longer there.

La Vagabonde was recognized as a major achievement immediately upon the book's publication. It was considered for the Goncourt Prize of 1911, although on the final ballot it received only two of the ten votes. Later, it was explained that most members of the jury had not yet read it. In the same way that Claudine prefigures the tomboyish girl of the 1920s, so Renée in some ways prefigures the career woman whose aspirations and frustrations have been a rich source of material for twentieth-century writers.

Renée may not have been ready to break out of her chrysalis, but Colette was fast emerging from hers. In 1908 she wrote her first play, *En Camarades*, a two-act comedy about adultery, and played the leading role in its first production the following year. Colette's dramatic works which, in addition to *En Camarades*, include stage adaptations of *La Vagabonde*, *Chéri*, and *Gigi*, a scenario for a ballet entitled *La Décapitée* (1935), and a libretto, *L'Enfant et les sortilèges* (1925), that was set to music by Ravel, add little to her stature as an artist. They do, however, show her unfailing interest in all aspects of the theater. The drama criticism she wrote for various French news-

papers from 1933 to 1938 (later collected in a stout
volume entitled *La Jumelle noire* (Black Opera
Glasses) is marked by an intimate knowledge of
stagecraft, a sympathetic understanding of the art of
acting, and by a novelist's flair for evoking the total
atmosphere of an evening in the theater.

Unlike Renée who refused Max's love, Colette
had accepted the love of Auguste Hériot, who served
as a model for Max. Apparently her affection for
Hériot was scarcely more than tepid. He was simply
one of the many lovers who slipped in and out of her
life without leaving much of a trace behind. In
December 1910, after finishing *La Vagabonde*, Colette joined the staff of the newspaper *Le Matin*. Her
entry into journalism did not, however, prevent her
from continuing her music-hall career, for she kept on
performing for some two and a half years, during
which time she also worked on a new novel. She continued to be associated with *Le Matin* until 1923,
serving at various times as reporter and writer, then
contributing editor and, for a time, literary editor.

In December 1912 Colette married Henry de
Jouvenel, who was three years her junior and then
co-editor-in-chief of *Le Matin*. Seven months later, at
the age of forty, she gave birth to a daughter whom
she was to write about frequently, calling her, as
Captain Colette had called his daughter, Bel-Gazou.
Colette's second husband was an aristocrat who owned
an ancestral castle and who, using his aristocratic and
journalistic connections, was to have a distinguished
career in politics. It reached a high point with his
appointment in 1933 as French ambassador to Rome.
Jouvenel's marriage to Colette, however, was one of
his less successful enterprises. Infidelities, probably

on both sides, made their relationship stormy, and in 1924 they were divorced.

The year 1913 was marked, not only by the birth of her daughter, but also by the publication of another novel, *L'Entrave* (published in English first as *Recaptured* and later as *The Shackle*) a sequel to *La Vagabonde* and a continuation of Renée's story. Like *La Vagabonde* and several of the later novels, *L'Entrave* was serialized in a weekly magazine before being published in book form. There was a bit of a race, Colette says, between the baby and the book. The baby won, and the magazine had to interrupt its serialization of the novel for several weeks before Colette found time to complete the book.

Colette later criticized the ending of *L'Entrave*, calling it lifeless and botched. It cannot be denied that the novel as a whole is less polished than *La Vagabonde* and that the final forty pages or so, ostensibly the account of perhaps the most intensely emotional experience in Renée's life, sometimes read like a scholastic disputation on the nature of love. Renée's terribly lucid and dry, clinical dissection of her own emotions makes her a somewhat less credible fictional character in *L'Entrave* than she had been in the earlier novel. The rather too facile opposition between independence and love, between the pleasures of sex and the sorrows of love, is so rigorously articulated, so neatly diagrammatic, that the ending of the novel is too pat to provide the kind of artistically satisfying resolution that marked the conclusion of *La Vagabonde*.

Still, *L'Entrave* is an essential book in the economy of Colette's work. "Heroism is not my forte," Colette once remarked. Nor was Renée's anguished rejection of love the forte of Colette's heroines. The Renée of *La Vagabonde* is in some respects the most heroic,

perhaps the most Cornelian of Colette's feminine characters. But Colette, who in 1912 found love again in
the person of Henry de Jouvenel, now leads Renée,
protesting though she is through much of the novel,
out of her isolation and into the arms of a man she
loves.

Renée is now three years older. A small inheritance has permitted her to quit the music hall. As the
novel opens, she is living in a hotel in Nice. The first
paragraph evokes the monotony, emptiness, grayness
and banality of her present life. Even the dark suit
she habitually wears blends in with the predominately
monochromatic tone of the novel. In *L'Entrave* Colette did what certain novelists in the nineteen fifties
and sixties strove to do, namely to create the flat
surface texture of a life that is essentially drab and
mediocre. Events are reduced to tropisms, to a series
of responses to trivial and apparently meaningless
incidents.

As at the beginning of *La Vagabonde*, it is winter. An occasional sunny day is followed by several
days of rain. A chance glimpse of Max, his wife and
child prompts Renée's "exhausting internal monologue"[35] which forms the heart of the novel. No longer
having the discipline of dancing or of writing to give
a structure to her life, for she seems to have abandoned writing as well as the music hall, Renée vaguely
feels the need to "revitalize" herself. Tired of the tatty
people she has met at the hotel and of the appalling
inanity of their conversation, but also mildly attracted
to one of them, Jean, Renée goes to Geneva. Once
again she flees from a potentially dangerous male,
although her flight is much less conscious than it was
in *La Vagabonde*.

The grayness and monotony of the Genevan

landscape in February corresponds to the creeping boredom of Renée's chaste, all-too-chaste, life. When Jean arrives in pursuit, the two begin moving around each other in a slow-paced dance that is the artistic high point of the book. In the analysis of love that follows, Colette separates that most tantalizing and complex of human emotions into two component parts: physical pleasure and what she calls "the rest." Eager for the former but afraid of the latter, Renée finally consents to become Jean's mistress, deceiving herself into believing that their relationship can be a purely physical involvement.

The last third of the novel is a demonstration of the fact that Renée's belief in her ability to separate pleasure from "the rest" is "a profound error."[36] Their springtime of sensual delight does not last long. If the Renée of *La Vagabonde* had a Cornelian streak in her character, the Renée of *L'Entrave* has at times a curiously Racinian air about her. Lucid and terrified, she watches herself as she moves slowly and inexorably toward love. Images of darkness, shadows, ruin and destruction color her somber reflections:

I weighed all the danger the day I began to despise what you [Jean] gave me: a joyful, facile pleasure that left me ungrateful, free and easy, a somewhat wild or fierce pleasure like hunger and thirst, and innocent as they are. One day I began to think of everything you did not give me; I moved into the chill shadow that stretches out in front of love.[37]

At first Renée resists the "total submission" that is love. During the troubled summer that she and Jean spend on the rugged coast of Brittany, she wanders alone, as in some Gethsemane, along "a thorny path" that leads to "a dungeon of rocks where the wind, like

her sorrow, lashes her."[38] Offended by Renée's unwill-
ingness to renounce her independence, Jean leaves
her. After a separation of two months, however, Renée
concludes that life without Jean is intolerable. She
calls him back and, by submitting to the servitude of
love, accepts the full burden of femininity.

In *La Vagabonde* Renée had refused Max
because she wanted "to possess through her own eyes
the wonders of the world."[39] At the end of *L'Entrave*
she agrees to see the world through Jean's eyes and,
in a tone that Colette later called derisively "the
approbative tone of a conclusion in which the characters do not believe,"[40] Renée views her submission as
the essential feature of a woman's love:

To get him, to tremble, fearing that he might escape from
me, to see him escape and then, patiently, to draw near
again in order to recapture him—from now on, that will
be my occupation, my mission. All that I loved before him
will then be restored to me: light, music, the rustling of
trees, the shy, fervent summons of tame animals, the proud
silence of men who are suffering—all these will be restored
to me, but *through* him and provided that I possess him
. . . I foolishly tried to pass over him, taking him for an
obstacle and not realizing that he was the limit of my
universe. I believe that many women at first make the
same mistake I did before assuming once again their place
which is *on this side* of a man.[41] [Colette's italics]

L'Entrave, written in the months following Colette's second marriage and during her pregnancy,
clearly records the author's attempt to come to grips
with her own feminine nature. Years before, Sido had
watched her young daughter trying to sew and had
sighed: "You will never look like anything but a boy
trying to sew."[42] Both Claudine and Renée share Colette's reluctance "to be only a woman." It must be

said that Colette's concept of "being a woman" is essentially the concept that prevailed in the French middle class of 1900. Psychologically rather than sociologically oriented, she saw in "being a woman" or in "being a man" two modes of existence whose origins lay in the very nature of things. Not unlike those hard-nosed French moralists of the seventeenth and eighteenth centuries who, in somber, crystalline aphorisms, distilled their thoughts about what is, not about what should be, Colette accepts her society's concepts of femininity and masculinity as a kind of natural law and never suggests that they may be culturally determined.

Renée's final submission to Jean, overstated and preachy as it is—a weakness in the novel's execution rather than in its conception—represents Colette's own reconciliation, or perhaps treaty, with man. Her subsequent heroines will never again struggle against their own femininity or try to rival men on their own ground. Although sparring between men and women continues to be the major theme of later novels, it becomes a kind of duel between feminine and masculine instincts as represented by a woman and a man, rather than a conflict between contrary instincts within one individual. In later novels, the characters themselves tend to become identified with the impersonal forces of female and male sexuality which they incarnate. Unlike Renée, whose inner conflict gives her a richness of character not always found in Colette's gallery of fictional heroines, many later protagonists tend to have little individual relief as they play out, allegorically, the drama of human sexuality. Many of them are curiously insubstantial and seem to vanish once the reader has closed the book. They slip from the memory as evasively as the melody of a Debussy

prelude. Instead of being unique characters with rich
and distinctive personalities, they are essentially vari-
ations of pre-individual types that are posited behind
them: the aging courtesan, the boy being introduced
to love, the jealous wife, etc. If Colette's art was in
any way colored by a lifetime's reading of Balzac, it
was perhaps in her concept of fictional characters, for
Balzac's novels, especially the early ones, are marked
by the Master's caricatural impulse—an impulse which
prompted him to see characters as destinies rather
than as individuals.

As a kind of final tribute to the music hall which
she left after the birth of her daughter, Colette collected her sketches of music-hall life and published
them in 1913 under the title of *L'Envers du music-hall*
(*Music-Hall Sidelights*). Pathetic, vulnerable, courageous, coarse, and often hungry, the performers,
behind their grease paint and tawdry costumes, tend
to lose their individual and sexual identities as they
work together as comrades. Despite the tinselly
dreams and the sordidness of the surroundings, they
remain singularly pure, dignified by their single-
minded dedication to their art. In *L'Envers du music-
hall,* as elsewhere in her books, Colette stresses the
redemptive power of work. Although there is no direct
social criticism in her fiction, there is an obvious cor-
relation between the idleness of the bourgeois characters in her novels and their incessant embroilment in
the impure world of love-making. It might be noted
in this respect that Renée becomes entrapped in love
only when she inherits some money and quits working.
    Several of Colette's portraits of acrobats and cir-
cus performers have the wistfully sad yet dignified

quality one sees in Picasso's famous paintings of harlequins and saltimbanques, done around 1905. Her brief depiction of a contortionist who smilingly endures excruciating pain while performing before an amused public suggests both the suffering and the triumph over suffering which, for Colette, characterize the lives of music-hall artists. Her description of a man who, terrified, risks his life daily by riding a bicycle on a turning disk that moves faster and faster has some of the intensity of Kafka's marvelous *In the Gallery* (1916–17), although it does not have the allegorical richness of Kafka's tale.

During World War I, Colette continued her career as a journalist, filing dispatches from Verdun, Rome and Paris. The sketches and chronicles she wrote during the war years, as well as those she wrote later, never deal with political or military matters. Some are cameo-like portraits of famous contemporaries. Others, such as her superb description of Venice in the summer of 1915, are descriptions of places she visited. Still others deal with subjects as varied as child rearing, feminine fashions, automobiles, and gardening. Regularly collected and published in book form, Colette's sundry articles are minor works. Still, they constitute a twentieth-century chronicle that is not without interest. And they often manage to evoke the hum of daily life, which was always what interested Colette most.

In 1919 Colette published another novel, *Mitsou, ou comment l'esprit vient aux filles* (Mitsou, or How Girls Grow Wise). Free of the purple patches that occasionally crop up in the novels about Claudine and Renée, *Mitsou* is considerably shorter than the previous novels. Its terse style and brevity indicate the direction that Colette's art was taking, for subsequent novels are invariably concise, often scarcely one hundred pages long.

In *Mitsou* Colette experimented for the only time in her writing career with fictional form and technique. The first section of the novel is presented partly in dramatic form, that is to say, it is printed as if it were a play containing nothing but dialogue and stage directions, and partly in the more usual narrative form. The increased importance of dialogue is significant, for Colette's succeeding novels tend to be reduced to dialogue, with just enough narrative content to sustain the conversation. The second section is composed of letters between Mitsou and a lieutenant.

Despite Proust's assertion, made in a letter to Colette, that he wept "a little" while reading *Mitsou*, the novel comes dangerously close at times to being sentimental.[43] Mitsou, a hard-working but thoroughly common music-hall girl, meets a handsome, fatuously bourgeois lieutenant dressed in blue. For Mitsou, it is love; for the blue lieutenant it is just another fling before going back to the front. Mitsou invites the lieutenant up to her apartment. When he arrives, she exclaims, like Agnès in Giroudoux's *L'Apollon de Bellac*: "How handsome you are!" After their one night together, the lieutenant leaves. The ensuing correspondence between the two clarifies the meaning of the subtitle, "How Girls Grow Wise." Mitsou's letters, which at first are rather awkward and laboriously written, full of errors both in grammar and spelling, become increasingly literary and elegant. It is the magic of love that has wrought this miracle. When Mitsou realizes that her blue lieutenant is not coming back to her, she informs him in her final letter, rather touchingly it must be admitted, that she is "going to become his illusion."[44]

Two aspects of the novel are worth noting in particular. Colette repeatedly describes Mitsou and the lieutenant, who are both twenty-four years old, as "very young." The lieutenant, especially, is described as if he were an adolescent. In subsequent novels, Colette becomes increasingly interested in adolescent or adolescent-like creatures who combine the physical graces of both sexes. Tending to reduce her characters to embodiments of instinctual urges, Colette often focuses on that moment when adolescents become conscious of their female or male sexuality, on that moment when their awareness of their nature begins to determine their actions and to shape their lives.

The other interesting feature in *Mitsou* is that in this novel Colette depicts a girl who is essentially shallow and vulgar, but who, when touched by love, can rise above her apparent limitations and "attain a level of banal heroism."[45] The capacity of a shallow, mediocre woman (and nearly all of Colette's heroines fall in this category) to transcend her own limitations through love is illustrated repeatedly in the lives of Colette's later heroines. Indeed, it is amply illustrated in the life of her next heroine, the formidable Léa in *Chéri*.

4

*The Novels
of Maturity*

In 1920 Colette was forty-seven years old. Her work as a journalist had taught her to observe the world around her more objectively than she might otherwise have been inclined to do and to record her observations as succinctly as possible. Her growing success as a writer was no doubt a source of deep satisfaction and gave her a sense of security which she had lacked earlier in her career. Age seems to have freed her from some of her anxieties about sex and to have resolved some of the problems—particularly that of independence versus submission—which had preoccupied her since her first marriage. Having mastered the craft of fiction and having forged a language perfectly suited to her literary aims, Colette was ready to embark on the most intensely creative period of her career.

Beginning around 1920, Colette's major works fall roughly into two categories: the first contains those novels for which she became famous in France and abroad; the second, those books of reminiscences and musings which, although they are not well known outside France, probably constitute her finest literary achievement. From about 1920 on, fiction and autobiography, which had been fused to form the content of most of Colette's early books, tend to be separated. The novels are still dominated by what I have called the constitutive symbol of Willy and continue, of course, to reflect facets of Colette's character and experience; but they are no longer fictional transpositions of Colette's own life in the way that the Claudine books and *La Vagabonde* were. In the books of a directly autobiographical nature, the constitutive symbol of Sido dominates. As Colette grows older, she writes more and more frequently about her mother, gradually fashioning year after year a glorious literary monument to Sido—a monument which, astonishingly, turns out to be Colette's own; for as Colette approaches the end of her long life, the "I" of her ruminations becomes indistinguishable from the figure of Sido. This figure of the author herself, ultimately consubstantial with Sido, is probably the most memorable literary figure to emerge from Colette's work.

As well as indicating the increasingly important role of crisp dialogue in Colette's fiction, *Mitsou* acquainted readers with a concept that reappears in *Chéri* (1920) as well as in later novels, giving them a certain structural similarity. The reader is first plunged into a world that is amazingly real in its physical concreteness. Colette's talent for evoking, in swift, telling strokes, the material aspect of ordinary things is remarkable. At first, the reality of this fictional world seems to be situated exclusively in materiality. Truth to the nature of things seems to mean truth to the physical order. In this world of objects dwell people who are shallow, vacuous, exasperatingly mediocre and complacent. Apparently devoid of any spiritual dimension, they are preoccupied with creature comforts and carnality.

Yet it would be inaccurate to say that Colette's fictional world is composed exclusively of physical elements. *Mitsou* is precisely the story of an evolution from physicality, from a kind of torpor to lucidity, self-awareness, dignity—in short, to "a level of banal heroism." The major novels of Colette's maturity trace, in one way or another, a movement that leads from crassness and materiality to some kind of heightened awareness. In both *Chéri* and *La Fin de Chéri* (*The Last of Chéri*), love and suffering, inseparable and indivisible, ultimately give an aura of dignity to characters who would otherwise be unbearably inane and smug.

The opening pages of *Chéri* are a prodigy of con-
densation and economy. They contain in embryo the
major themes of the novel as well as the symbols that
will bear the weight of the book's meaning. The novel
opens with the imperious voice of an unidentified
speaker: "Léa, give it to me, give me your pearl necklace! Do you hear me, Léa? Give me your pearls!"[1]
No answer is heard from the large iron bed that dominates the room. Suddenly, in a soft flutter of lace two
magnificent arms rise languidly from the sea of white
linen. The splendid limbs belong to the forty-nine-
year-old Léa, a superbly preserved courtesan who,
after a highly successful career during which she
amassed a considerable fortune, now lives with the
twenty-five-year-old Chéri.

Every detail in the opening pages is significant.
The beautiful pearl necklace which Chéri, like the
spoiled child he is, asks for so impatiently, belongs to
Léa who no longer wears it at night for fear that in
the morning light it might draw attention to her neck
which is beginning to wrinkle. Indeed, Léa is on the
brink of old age, a fact she realizes dimly but which
is masked by the presence of her young lover and by
her intense effort to create a luxurious, perfectly
ordered, and changeless world about her. The huge
bed, solid and apparently indestructible, is symbolic
of Léa herself, practical, passionately attached to
order and decorum, and totally imperturbable. "Luxe,
calme et volupté" reign in her bedroom which is
bathed in a peculiarly warm, rose-tinted light, creating a sense of well-being and enchantment that are
associated with Léa throughout the novel. Sensible
and down-to-earth, Léa is no doubt the ideal specimen
of a type, i.e., the successful demimondaine of around
1900.

Léa's impassiveness and monumentality are in sharp contrast to Chéri's nervousness, his agitation, irresponsibility and childishness. With consummate skill Colette combines in intricate contrapuntal patterns the grave yet vibrant melody that identifies Léa and the feverish, restless melody that characterizes Chéri. Chéri is first seen outlined against the rose-colored curtains that cover the window of Léa's bedroom. Against the morning sunlight, he is merely a shadow, and looks like "a graceful demon capering about against a furnace of light."[2] There is, in fact, something demonic about him. Very rich and extraordinarily handsome, he possesses a kind of satanic beauty that casts a spell on most of the women he meets. But he pays a price for his beauty: "His whole being breathed forth the melancholy of perfect works of art."[3] Writing about Chéri in 1946, Colette referred to "his melancholy which finally draws him toward a barren purity."[4] The beautiful pearl necklace represents the purity to which Chéri dimly aspires and the absolute which he vaguely and unconsciously identifies with his love for Léa.

In a flashback, Colette recounts the history of their liaison. It had begun during the summer of 1906 when Léa was forty-three and Chéri nineteen. Léa's initial interest in Chéri was protective and maternal. Having known him since he was an infant, she had proposed that he accompany her on a trip to Normandy where she hoped that fresh air and wholesome food would cure him of his restlessness and boredom. A kiss aroused their senses and changed the nature of the relationship between them. Rather, it added another dimension to their relationship, for Léa, although she became his mistress, remained protective and maternal; and Chéri, whose own mother was a hard-nosed former courtesan, found in Léa not only a mistress but, for the first time in his life, the warmth of maternal love.

Six years have passed and Chéri is about to be married off to a beautiful eighteen-year-old heiress, Edmée. Both Léa and Chéri view the approaching marriage with equanimity, for neither yet realizes the depth of his love for the other. The wedding takes place early in the autumn of 1912. The central part of the novel is composed of a diptych: Léa without Chéri and later Chéri without Léa.

Chéri leaves Paris for a six-month honeymoon trip. Once again Colette very discreetly uses seasonal changes to emphasize changing emotional states. The approach of winter not only foreshadows Léa's life without Chéri, but also her approaching old age. In fact, Léa is soon forced to face squarely both the reality of Chéri's absence and that of her own physical decline.

Paying a social call one day, she meets three former friends, aging courtesans all, and is struck by their grotesqueness, absurdity and repulsiveness. Indeed, Colette depicts them in undeniably caricatural terms. When the senile seventy-year-old Lili, dressed in the latest fashion and covered with jewels, hobbles into the room on her swollen legs, accompanied by her frail, stupid seventeen-year-old lover, Léa, after the customary greetings, leaves the room, repelled. She has looked into the future and seen what she, too, might become. Feeling a bit ill, she goes to bed as soon as she gets home. "Suddenly a feeling of pain so sharp that she at first thought it was physical made her jump up, contorted her mouth and tore from her, as she gasped hoarsely, a sob and a name: "Chéri'!"[5] Practical as always, she takes her temperature. When she sees that it is normal and that her ailment is therefore not physiological, she moves into action, hoping to cure herself of the ache of loneliness. She leaves Paris for the winter and tells no one where she will be or when she will return.

In early spring Chéri and Edmée return to Paris. It is plain that their marriage is not going well. Chéri who, at the beginning of the novel, was selfish and malicious enough to qualify for the epithet of spoiled brat, now suffers for the first time in his life. Unable to face life without Léa, he leaves his wife, moves into a hotel, and frequents an opium den where he stares at the fake pearls which a decrepit habituée wears. Incapable of coping with reality alone, he simply waits for Léa to return. And return she does, in late spring. Aware of the fact that Léa is back in Paris, Chéri bursts into the rose-tinted bedroom one midnight and announces that he has come home. After her initial displeasure, Léa, in a paroxysm of gratitude and devotion, falls into the arms of her lover, friend and prodigal son.

For a few brief hours they delude themselves into thinking that things can be the same and that they can pick up where they left off. The next morning, however, Chéri, pretending to be still asleep, observes Léa as she moves about the room making arrangements for their flight from Paris; intoxicated with happiness, she believes that the two of them can abandon everything and live together in some idyllic hideaway in the south. For a moment Chéri sees her, not through the eyes of love, but through the impartial eyes of an objective spectator. He sees an aging woman with a double chin and gnarled neck muscles; he glimpses a truth that swiftly and unconsciously alters his attitude toward her.

When, a few minutes later, he says "You were for
me . . . ," Léa immediately hears the past tense; her
hopes for happiness come crashing down, for Chéri
has relegated her to the past. At first she rebels and,
trying to hurt him, lashes out unjustly at Edmée.
However, as Chéri, in a paean of praise, describes
the Léa he still loves (an idealized Léa who, alas,
now exists only in his own heart), the real Léa gradually renounces any claim on him and, like Mitsou,
consents to be his illusion. Transcending the limitations of her nature, Léa, whose whole life has been
devoted to a calculated pursuit of pleasure, sacrifices
her own happiness and gently sends Chéri back to his
wife and his youth. As she glances in the mirror, her
heart sinking, she sees the image of a fat, old woman
—an image which she must now accept as a faithful
reflection of herself.

That she does accept this image of herself is precisely the gesture that raises her to the level of banal
heroism. It is one of Colette's basic beliefs, derived no
doubt from her lucid awareness of the strengths and
limitations of her own character, that "women are
solid," that they, being somehow closer to and more
in harmony with the elemental forces of life than
men, have a limitless capacity to adapt and adjust, to
face reality squarely and to cope with it honestly and
sensibly. Only Colette's feminine characters are
endowed with this talent. Creating a fictional world
that is inhabited by women who possess no moral or
intellectual qualities of distinction, Colette affirms that
women, even those who seem shallow and vulgar
when judged by standards that men might apply to
them, possess "an elastic will, a desire to live and to
command, in short, the prodigious and female apti-
tude for happiness."[6] Léa learns to live happily with-

out Chéri; Chéri cannot adapt to life without Léa. That is the subject of the sequel Colette wrote to *Chéri*.

La Fin de Chéri was published six years after *Chéri*. The action takes place in the summer and fall of 1919. With her usual talent for evoking time and place, Colette depicts a society whose values have been disrupted by the war. It is a society that has just discovered jazz and whiskey, a changing society in which young men and women, making up for four or five years of deprivation, strive frantically to enjoy life, to get rich, and to move ahead. Against this background of bustle and self-interest, stands Chéri, as handsome and idle as ever. A decorated war-hero (his heroism was purely accidental), he is now thirty-two years old. His wife, Edmée, and his mother, Charlotte, dressed in stiff, white hospital uniforms or in smartly tailored military uniforms are whirlwinds of activity. Administrators in a military hospital, they rush from home to hospital to General Headquarters; curt, efficient and supremely self-congratulatory, they are involved in all sorts of grandiose schemes which require endless meetings with people in high places, especially American generals. The adjective Colette uses repeatedly to evoke their world is white—a color which, with its connotations of coldness and sterility, contrasts sharply to the warm rose color that characterized Léa's world. Chéri, who was rich before the war, is now immensely wealthy; Edmée and Charlotte have shrewdly managed his fortune and in fact continue to do so even after his return.

Stated in the broadest terms, *La Fin de Chéri* chronicles Chéri's inability to come to grips with life and his final despair which leads him to suicide. The subject is stark in its simplicity. With considerable skill, Colette, displaying the classical virtue of restraint, records Chéri's half-hearted and futile attempts to give meaning to his life. As each attempt fails, he slips closer to suicide. The story moves forward with such rigorous logic that the final resolution, with its tragic inevitability, brings with it a sense of release akin to that felt at the end of a good tragedy.

Early in the novel, notions of decline and futility are associated with Chéri. Having nothing to do, or rather, as his mother tells him gruffly, having never learned to do anything but lead the life of a gigolo, he gradually begins to think about Léa: "He would awaken somewhere outside the present, stripped of his most recent past, taken back to the time of his youth —back to Léa."[7]

It has frequently been pointed out that Chéri's malaise, his dissatisfaction with life, is akin to the nausea which existential heroes such as Sartre's Roquentin and Camus' Meursault experience some ten or fifteen years later. Indeed, Chéri, speaking to his mother, uses a term that later becomes a feature of the Sartrean vocabulary; trying to explain his dislike for people in general, he says: "They're all bastards" (*salauds*).[8] However, Chéri's nausea, unlike Roquentin's, does not have a metaphysical dimension. A result of a unique and, Colette insists, abnormal psychological makeup, it is as exceptional as are Chéri's beauty and wealth.

In a supreme attempt to escape the world of *salauds*, Chéri returns to Léa, hoping to rediscover the womb-like security of her rose-colored bedroom. The meeting between the two is the high point of the book. As he approaches the door of Léa's new apartment, Chéri hears a ripple of laughter and realizes that she is not alone. Entering the room, he sees two figures: a woman dressed in black who is obviously paying a social call, and an enormously fat woman with gray hair who has her back turned to him. "Where is Léa?" he wonders. Suddenly, the fat woman turns around and Chéri, stunned, recognizes Léa's sparkling blue eyes. The ensuing conversation, both funny and sad, is masterfully written. The credibility of this scene, and indeed of the entire novel, depends on Colette's ability to pace Chéri's emotional collapse in such a way that it seems logical and ineluctable. She succeeds admirably well. Looking at the old, ruddy-faced lady before him, Chéri is tormented by the thought that this "placid disaster," as Colette calls her, is indeed the Léa he loves. He can scarcely refrain from crying out: "Stop! Show me your real self! Throw off your disguise!"[9]

Not only does the former Léa fail to reappear, she no longer exists. It is not Léa's physical transformation that Chéri finds most intolerable; it is the fact that Léa has wholeheartedly accepted her present state, that she has become a kind of jolly, virile old lady for whom the joys and sorrows of love are now a closed book. She and Chéri no longer speak the same language. Seeing that Chéri looks ill, Léa tells him solicitously that he should have his urine analyzed. Like the parish priest in *Madame Bovary* who, completely unaware of the nature of Emma's anguish, advises her to drink a cup of tea, Léa gives Chéri the address of a little bistro she knows about and tells him to take better care of his stomach. Suddenly, Chéri notices that Léa is wearing her magnificent pearl necklace. "They haven't changed!" he thinks. "They and I are unchanged."[10]

Life, however, is characterized by change. No doubt Chéri's friend, Desmond, is right when he tells

him that he should work: "Work is a great way of getting back on your feet, pal."[11] But Chéri is totally
lacking in the will to work. Mediocre, weak and
spineless as he may be, he is not, however, completely
responsible for his plight. As in a tragedy, the hero is
caught in a web from which he cannot escape. From
the very beginning of *Chéri*, Colette cunningly
alluded to Chéri's childhood and adolescence in such
a way that his adult behavior is credible. Léa, too, is
partly to blame for Chéri's inability to grow up; she
kept him at her feet for six years, weaving around him
a magic world—the only one in which he can survive.
Edmée, who scornfully rejects Chéri's suggestion that
they have a child, also shares the responsibility for her
husband's suicide. "Edmée never realized," notes Colette, "that the feminine appetite for possession tends
to emasculate any living conquest, and can reduce a
magnificent and inferior male to the status of a courtesan."[12]

As Chéri moves closer and closer to suicide, the
weather becomes "precociously autumnal." "Winter
will come soon,"[13] he thinks as he watches dark rain
clouds move across the late September sky. In a bar
he once again runs into La Copine, the old opium-
smoking courtesan whose fake pearls he had stared
at for hours on end when, years before, he had sought
to console himself for Léa's temporary absence from
Paris. Dressed in black, La Copine is compared to one
of the Fates and, unwittingly, precipitates Chéri's
death. Her apartment, which is described as being a
"black hole," is full of photographs of Léa when she
···   ;. Chéri spends hours looking at them. Faith-
            impossible (and no doubt childish) ideal,
            ⁄ picks up La Copine's revolver and, lying
            ont of Léa's image, shoots himself.

It is apparent that Colette approved of Léa's renunciation of love and of her frank acceptance of old age as an inevitable part of life. She sympathized with but clearly condemned Chéri's suffering. Writing in 1928, three years after the beginning of her happy liaison with Maurice Goudeket, a dealer in pearls, seventeen years her junior, whom she would marry in 1935, Colette wrote that suffering because of love, although painful, is childish:

Suffering is perhaps childish, an undignified preoccupation; I mean to say suffering because of a man when one is a woman, or because of a woman when one is a man. It is extremely painful. I admit that it is barely tolerable. But I am very much afraid that this kind of suffering is unworthy of any consideration.[14]

Yet Chéri represents a facet of Colette's experience as surely as Léa represents Colette's facing up to old age. Colette understood only too well Chéri's intense nostalgia for a warm, rose-colored room, dominated by the presence of a maternal figure. She herself had experienced that nostalgia during her years of marriage to Willy and again during the years of her lonely music-hall career. She, too, carried within her heart the image of a past that was pure and changeless. In fact, in 1922, two years after the publication of *Chéri* and four years before the publication of *La Fin de Chéri*, Colette published *La Maison de Claudine*, the first of those memorable books in which she lovingly resuscitates her childhood, her family, and especially her mother, transforming her own image of the past into art of exceptional strength and beauty.

Colette spent the summers of 1921 and 1922 in a villa on the coast of Brittany. With her were her eight-

year-old daughter and two teen-aged step-sons, Ber-
trand and Renaud de Jouvenel. Freed for a few weeks
from her duties as literary editor of *Le Matin*, Colette
worked on a new novel. Although *Le Blé en herbe*
(*Ripening Seed*) is not autobiographical, it no doubt
reflects in some way the mood of those summers, for
the novel is set on the Breton coast and the protagonists are two adolescents.

On July 29, 1922, *Le Matin* began serializing
Le Blé en herbe, publishing chapters at irregular
intervals. By March 31, 1923, fifteen chapters had
been published, all of about the same length. The
editors then learned that in the final chapters Colette
intended to have the hero, sixteen-and-a-half-year-old
Philippe, and the heroine, fifteen-and-a-half-year-old
Vinca, make love. Incensed, they refused to continue
publication. No longer compelled to divide the
remainder of her novel into chapters of predeter-
mined length, Colette wrote a long final chapter full
of events she had no doubt intended to space out in
several smaller chapters. Artistically, the effect is curiously satisfying. Events throughout the first fifteen
chapters are spaced evenly, creating a sense of steady
but deliberate progression which is in perfect accord
with the emotional state of the protagonists. In the
last chapter, events occur swiftly, unchecked by chapter divisions; the quickening of the narrative under-
scores nicely the heightened emotional tone and the
increased intensity of the drama as it draws to a
close.

The story is simple: For some fifteen years
Philippe and Vinca have spent their summers playing
together on the Breton coast where their parents share
a villa. This summer, however, the relationship between
them has subtly changed, for Phil has begun to be

aware of his masculinity, and Vinca, of her femininity. "All their childhood united them, adolescence separated them,"[15] notes Colette on the second page of the novel. On the threshold of love (Colette's original title for the novel was *Le Seuil*, The Threshold), Phil and Vinca are a latter-day Daphnis and Chloë. Phil, like Daphnis, is initiated into the mysteries of love by an older woman, Mme Dalleray, the "Lady in White."

With a kind of feminine instinct, Vinca senses the presence of a rival. Waiting until after Mme Dalleray has returned to Paris, Vinca accuses Phil of infidelity and betrayal. A few weeks before, in the idyllic world of childhood, she had wished to die with Phil; like Chéri, for whom death was the only means of preserving an illusion cruelly refuted by reality, Vinca had felt instinctively that death would be the apotheosis of an innocent, childish love threatened by the approach of adulthood. Now however, forced into the role of a woman by her awareness of a rival, she no longer wants to die; instead she assumes what Colette, basing her judgment on her own experience, calls a woman's mission: "the mission to endure, vested in the female of every species, and the imperious instinct to settle into unhappiness by exploiting it like a rich mine of precious ore." Vinca now "fights in her primitive way to save the couple."[16] Within the framework of the story, she succeeds; she and Phil spend the night together; both now enter the turbulent world of adult love. In none of Colette's other novels do the principal characters so clearly represent the author's image of Man and Woman, adversaries who are pitted against each other in accordance with the laws of love.

For Chéri, Léa's rose-colored bedroom represented the chrysalis of childhood from which he refused to

emerge. For Phil and Vinca, childhood is represented
by the warm, bright, sunny days spent on the beach
in innocent and boisterous comradeship. As is usual
in Colette's major novels, details in *Le Blé en herbe*
are seldom gratuitous; each contributes to the overall
atmosphere, and Colette's sensual evocations of the
sea, sky and sand are indeed skillful. That Phil and
Vinca are at the end of their childhood and innocence
is underscored by the fact that the story begins toward
the end of August as the holidays draw to a close.
Despite the limpid blue and yellow tones that dominate the bright scene, there are intimations of shadows
and of a darkening landscape. September brings rainy
days and preparations for the return to Paris at the
end of the month. The approach of autumn, as inexorable as the change from childhood to maturity, foreshadows the suffering which Phil and Vinca will soon
encounter and which, Colette believes, is an integral
part of love. In the first chapter Vinca (nicknamed
Pervenche, or Periwinkle, because of her blue eyes)
hunts for shrimp in a bright, clear pool; suddenly
"Phil's shadow darkens the sunny pool." Colette's
chiaroscuro, a technique she uses deftly throughout
Le Blé en herbe, is charged with symbolic meaning.

Mme Dalleray introduces a contrasting tonality
into the color scheme of the novel. Constantly
described as virile, her first name is Camille, an
"asexual name"[17] Colette notes, for it may be a man's
as well as a woman's. Like Renaissance poets who,
imitating Petrarch, frequently used oxymorons such as
"burning cold" and "freezing heat" to suggest the contradictory nature of love, Colette reverts (probably
unconsciously) to similar formulas and envelops Mme
Dalleray in an atmosphere that is both frigid and
sultry. Her white dress, her diamonds, the ice cubes in

the drink she offers Phil, all create an impression of hardness and coldness reinforced by her mordant comments and impenetrable smile. In contrast to Mme Dalleray herself, is the room into which she invites Phil: red, white, black and gold are the dominant colors; heavy curtains cut out the light, creating an atmosphere of mystery and voluptuousness; the presence of a large red and blue parrot adds an exotic touch to the décor. As he drinks the orangeade offered him, Phil feels "the cold drink burn his throat"[18] and hears Mme Dalleray's "little demonic laugh."

Indeed, Mme Dalleray is like one of those spirits in fairy tales: she suddenly appears before the protagonists, performs her task, then vanishes. She is the instrument that tears open the chrysalis of childhood which enveloped Phil and Vinca. Having lost the happiness of childhood, they acquire adult knowledge and learn that love, in Colette's words, is composed of "a bit of pain and a bit of pleasure."[19]

After the publication of *La Fin de Chéri* in 1928, Colette wrote only four more works that may unhesitatingly be called novels: *La Seconde* (1929), *La Chatte* (1933), *Duo* (1934) and *Julie de Carneilhan* (1941). She did, however, publish several volumes of short stories which develop themes similar to those found in her longer fictional works: *La Femme cachée* (1924), *Bella-Vista* (1937), *Chambre d'hôtel* (1940) and the most famous of all because of the world-wide success of its title story, *Gigi* (1944).

During the 1920s Colette began fashioning her image of Sido. Nowhere is the opposition between the constitutive symbols of Sido and Willy more apparent than in Sido's declaration that the love one reads about in novels is a lot of stuff and nonsense. And yet the separation between the worlds of Sido and Willy is not complete, for they meet in the person of Colette. From *Mitsou* on, all of Colette's fictional heroines are subtly influenced by the figure of Sido. Léa's capacity to endure and to enjoy is derived from Sido. Vinca's discovery that the suffering she endures for Phil is a rich mine of experience is derived from Sido's love for Captain Colette. Although *La Seconde* (*The Other One*) is undoubtedly one of Colette's least successful novels, it too illustrates the theme of feminine adaptability and endurance which is ultimately best exemplified in the figure of Sido and in that of Sido's daughter, Colette herself.

Reverting to the claustrophobic, harem-like atmosphere of the last three Claudine books, Colette evokes the vacuous life of plump Fanny, married to Farou, a popular playwright and an indefatigable woman-chaser, and of Jane, Farou's English secretary. The crux of the drama is Fanny's discovery that Jane is. Farou's mistress. Although Fanny initially views Jane as a rival, she soon accepts her as an accomplice. Each of the two women needs the gentle presence of the other; together they create a little island of comfort and serenity in the midst of Farou's hustle and bustle.

No doubt Fanny's acceptance of a *ménage à trois* is intended to illustrate a kind of "banal heroism." Jane refers to Fanny's "superiority which consisted in putting Farou at the disposal of every woman."[20] But Fanny, singularly bovine and sluggish, seems to act from weakness of character rather than from conviction. Instead of being heroic, she is simply feckless.

Farou, with his peremptory tone, numerous mistresses, and incessant literary and theatrical activities, reminds one of Willy. Moreover, the complicity between Fanny and Jane is strangely reminiscent of an event in Colette's early life, for in *Mes Apprentis-sages* she explains that sometime after learning of Willy's affair with Charlotte Kinceler, she befriended "Lotte" out of curiosity; occasionally, the three of them would meet. Whether or not Colette was aware of these echoes from her past, one cannot know; or rather, one cannot know at the present time, for Colette's correspondence is still largely unpublished. Despite the publication of six volumes of letters, it will no doubt be many years before anything like her complete correspondence is made public.

Like *La Seconde*, which precedes it, and *Duo*, which follows it, *La Chatte* (The Cat) is a variation on the theme of jealousy. One of Colette's most compact novels, it operates on several levels.

On the purely narrative level, it is a taut drama as full of suspense as a murder mystery: Twenty-four-year-old Alain, heir to a family business that is gently declining, marries Camille (once again Colette uses that "asexual name") who is the daughter of a family that has only recently acquired wealth. Waiting for their new home to be built, Alain and Camille move into the apartment of a friend who has left Paris for the three summer months. In fact, the number three, or the notion of triangularity, is a leitmotif that runs throughout the novel. The apartment is on the ninth floor, the tops of the three poplar trees that grow in the garden below are even with the apartment's three terraces, and, most important of all, the curiously shaped bedroom has three walls and is repeatedly referred to as "the triangular bedroom." When Alain brings his beautiful cat, Saha, to live with them, he creates a *ménage à trois*, and Camille gradually grows jealous of her rival. One evening when Alain is gone, she pushes Saha off the balcony.

Colette's description of this attempted murder (the cat's fall is broken by an awning) is a masterpiece of perfectly controlled writing. Slowly, Camille begins to pace back and forth across the narrow balcony, forcing the cat to jump from the railing to the floor and back to the railing. Saha, suddenly realizing that she is in mortal danger, utters a long, anguished meow and then falls silent as she intently watches her tormentor. Camille seems to tire first and glances at her watch; Saha relaxes her guard; suddenly, Camille thrusts her arms forward and pushes the cat off the railing. This is probably the most intensely dramatic scene Colette ever wrote.

When Alain brings Saha back up to the apartment, the cat stares at Camille in horror and hatred, accusing her in language that is mute but unmistakably clear. Little by little Alain realizes the truth. Leaving Camille, he and Saha return to the old family house and the lovely shaded garden where they were so happy before Alain's marriage.

On another level, the novel illustrates once again Colette's view that men and women are fundamentally incompatible. The hostility which Colette considers to be the normal relationship between the sexes is latent from the beginning of the novel. Alain and Camille are different in every respect, and if they come together it is for the only reason that men and women ever come together in Colette's world: sex. Alain is blond; Camille, brunette. Alain is passionately attached to his old house and garden; Camille is contemptuous of them as well as of the doddering servant who has been with Alain and his mother for years. Fond of jazz and fast sports cars, Camille is all slick modernity. Like Edmée, Chéri's wife, she is vulgarly materialistic. She is delighted with the little apartment, its glass and concrete walls, its vertiginous view of Parisian rooftops. Alain, on the other hand, finds it an "inhuman" place to live. Camille's eagerness for sex, her lack of modesty, in short, her feminine "impurity" shock Alain. With alarm he notices that he is getting thinner whereas Camille is putting on weight. Speaking to himself, he mutters what Colette calls "the age-old male grievance: She's getting fat on lovemaking. She's getting fat on me."[21] Alain searches for the "origin of their incompatibility" and finds it, not in their individual characters, but in the very nature of the relationship between men and women: "He returned to those retreats where the hostility of man to woman keeps its unaging freshness."[22] This is perhaps a warped view; nevertheless, it is one of the formal conventions that underlies all of Colette's fiction.

Saha is everything that Camille is not. With extraordinary skill, Colette evokes the grace, beauty and mystery of the blue-gray cat whose love for Alain, contrary to Camille's, is completely disinterested. Unlike Camille, Saha belongs to an elite race; she moves in a world of purity that is inaccessible to Camille. Uprooted and unhappy, Alain and Saha go out on the balcony one dawn while Camille is still asleep. For Colette, dawn is always the hour of purity, just as blue, a color she once called more mental than optical,[23] evokes the ideal. There, in the blue-gray dawn, the two exiles yearn to return to the paradise they have lost.

The third level of meaning is now apparent. Alain, like Chéri, refuses to abandon the kingdom of childhood as represented by the house and garden in

which he has lived all his life. The archetype of
Alain's house and garden is of course Sido's home in
Saint-Sauveur. Colette endows the old house and the
mysterious garden to which Alain is so irresistibly
attached with the peculiar poetic beauty she reserves
for evocations of the house in which she herself grew
up. The queen of Alain's kingdom is Saha. "Saha,"
says Alain's mother to her son, "is your illusion."[24]

At the end of the novel, Camille accuses Alain of
being a monster; from one point of view she is perfectly right. His attachment to an impossible ideal,
represented by the lost paradise of childhood, is a
monstrous denial of the present and of the future. It
is, moreover, too childish an ideal to elicit a sympathetic response in most readers. Alain's quarrel with the
world, like Chéri's, remains at too infantile a level to
merit much respect.

Colette's heroines, it may be argued, show greater
maturity, for they adjust to life and, after disappointment or a catastrophe, pick up the pieces and go on.
Camille, at the end of *La Chatte*, walks away from her
husband, making plans for her future, already organizing her life without Alain. But in Colette's world a
prerequisite for this admittedly admirable quality
seems to be a kind of coarseness—represented, for
example, by Camille's stubby, unattractive fingers—an
insensitiveness, a desire to dominate, and "an exclusively feminine immorality,"[25] as Colette notes in *La
Chatte*, that characterize virtually all her heroines.
Like Charlotte in *Le Pur et l'impur*, they all seem to
"despise that mental domain which bears a red, vis-
ceral name: the heart."[26] In *La Chatte* it is Saha
who has a heart, not Camille. The difference between
the two females is not only one of "quality," to use
Alain's term; it is the difference between the absence

of sex and its presence, between purity and impurity. "I have endowed my heroes with my most persistent phantoms,"[27] wrote Colette in 1941. If the novels deal primarily with what Colette repeatedly calls "the impure," her books of reminiscences, written alternately with the novels of her maturity, deal with "the pure."

Like a Two-Part Invention by Bach, *Duo* is composed of two voices—one a man's, the other a woman's. Although in virtually all the novels of her maturity Colette tends to present her characters in such a way that they incarnate the instinctual and antagonistic forces of male and female sexuality, in none is the confrontation between these two forces more clearly, more clinically presented than in *Duo*. Even more than in her other novels, Colette here generalizes about masculinity and femininity, writing numerous phrases such as: "entirely devoid of imagination, like most men";[28] "a woman's frankness of speech";[29] "playing to the gallery, like all men";[30] "the female desire to grovel and beg forgiveness";[31] "masculine susceptibility."[32]

But *Duo* is not only a duet; it is also a duel that ends in the death of the male protagonist. It traces the devastating effects of jealousy on Michel who accidentally learns that his wife, Alice, has had a brief love affair with one of his business associates, a certain Ambrogio. Images of disintegration, deterioration and crumbling are woven into the novel from its opening pages and reappear constantly, emphasizing the growing misunderstanding between the couple and Michel's slow descent into suicide. The country house in which they are spending the Easter holidays is gently falling into ruin: every time there is a storm,

more tiles blow off the roof; the window sills are rot-
ting; plates, tea pots and cups are broken at various
times throughout the novel; Michel's cigarette burns a
hole in the worm-eaten wood of his desk. And in the
distance a mist rises from the swollen river which
looks like a ribbon of land that has been stripped of
its vegetation and strewn with cinders.

As the novel opens, Michel is returning from a
morning inspection of his property. He crosses the
threshold, leaving behind the sunny out-of-doors, and
enters the somber house. Unwittingly he is also leaving behind him his ten years of happily married life,
for shortly after he goes inside he discovers a letter
proving his wife's infidelity. The remainder of the
novel consists essentially of the tortured conversations
that take place between Michel and Alice during the
next several days. An intermittent rain often accompanies their increasingly discordant duo.

The dissension between Michel and Alice is not
due to lack of love. Rather, it is due to the fact that in
Colette's world a male and a female are doomed by a
kind of biological fatality to perceive reality differ-
ently. For Alice, her three-week love affair was a
"dirty dream" of absolutely no consequence. Like all
of Colette's heroines, she lives in the present. Wishing
to save her marriage and "pick up the pieces,"[33] she
tells Michel that she never loved Ambrogio; she was
simply attracted to him momentarily by an imperious
sexual desire that was soon appeased; the affair meant
nothing to her. Instead of calming Michel's torment,
this knowledge increases his distress, for now he is
haunted by images of a lustful Alice in Ambrogio's
arms.

Unlike Alice, Michel does not try to salvage their
marriage. On the contrary, he luxuriates in his suffer-

ing with a kind of fatuous complacency and ostentatious self-esteem that Colette chooses to call masculine. Unable, as Colette's men usually are, to face
reality honestly, Michel is obsessed both by a sense of
irreparable loss and by a keen histrionic sense of the
role he should play as the betrayed husband. One gray
dawn (again Colette evokes the hour of purity) he
quietly walks into the river and drowns.

Curiously, the novel contains within itself a mini-
ature reflection of its own basic themes, for the relationship between the servant, Maria, and her husband
is a condensed version of the relationship between
Alice and Michel. When Alice notices a blistered burn
on Maria's arm and asks her how she hurt herself,
Maria answers that her husband hit her with a poker:
"He was getting his revenge," she explains. To Alice's
startled "Why?" Maria answers: "Just because he's my
man and I'm his woman. That's reason enough."[34]

Numerous commentators have asserted that Colette approves of Alice and condemns Michel. If one
considers Colette's total work, one may indeed assume
that she would find Alice's attitude more reasonable
and understandable than Michel's. (Indeed, Colette
defines Michel's love for Alice as "unreasonable."[35])
And yet, one of the strengths of the novel is that
Colette does not blame or condone. Even Alice's "mission to endure" is not presented as an admirable character trait; it is instinctual, and Alice can be neither
praised nor blamed for it.

Imbued with a sense of tragic inevitability, the
seemingly petty domestic drama between Alice and
Michel transcends the banality and mediocrity of the
characters and becomes a portentous confrontation
between man and woman, two adversaries who, in

Colette's world, are destined to misunderstand each
other.

In 1939 Colette published *Le Toutounier*, a short
work of scarcely sixty pages. It is a sequel to *Duo*
and serves as a kind of coda to the longer work.

After the death of Michel, Alice returns to the
tiny shabby Parisian apartment which is home to her
and to two of her sisters who still live there. The principal pieces of furniture in the apartment are an old
grand piano and an immense leather sofa which Alice
and her sisters call the *toutounier*. By extension,
toutounier refers to the apartment itself. The French
word *toutou* means dog in the language of children.
Indeed, when Alice and her sisters cuddle up on the
old family sofa they are not unlike three puppies seeking warmth and security in physical proximity. But the
toutounier, as well as being a kind of kennel into
which Alice and her sisters may crawl when the
stresses of the outside world become too great, also
represents a link with the past; it signifies the refuge
of childhood. An exclusively feminine world, the small
apartment is a sanctuary from which the cherished
enemy, man, is excluded.

The tone of the novel is correspondingly girlish
and feminine. Although the sisters range in age from
twenty-nine to thirty-seven, their language is full of
vapid schoolgirl argot and chatter that may well strike
a reader as an unpleasant affectation. Moreover, in an
attempt to charge the atmosphere of the novel with
an exclusively feminine presence, Colette repeatedly
refers to the sisters' legs, arms, eyes, hips, to their
various odors, and to their breasts which pop out of
their negligees rather more frequently than one might
reasonably expect.

Having been brought up in the school of hard

knocks, Alice and her sisters know that the *toutounier* is only a temporary refuge, a kind of recharging station at which they periodically stop before going back into the fray. When her two sisters decide to follow their lovers and leave Paris, Alice chooses to remain in the apartment; she will keep the *toutounier* intact so that they will be able to return to it in their hour of need just as she has done.

Colette's last novel is also about going back. Published in 1941 when Colette was approaching seventy and already suffering from the arthritis which would soon paralyze her for the rest of her life, *Julie de Carneilhan* reveals a technical skill and a mastery of understatement that are remarkable.

Julie, a forty-five-year-old aristocrat, is relatively poor, tough and rather disagreeably arrogant. Like many of Colette's heroines, she affects cynicism and a certain hard-boiledness. Since her divorce from her second husband, Herbert d'Espivant, who in some ways resembles Colette's second husband, she lives in a small studio apartment. Although Julie has a twenty-eight-year-old lover, her life is essentially empty. Her only friends are two or three rather vulgar companions with whom she goes to the cinema or occasionally to a bar. That she is superior to her circumstances and to the company she keeps is suggested by an image that reappears throughout the novel: both Julie and her brother, whose nobility goes back several centuries, are compared to thoroughbred horses. In particular, Colette frequently alludes to their sensitive nostrils and to their lean, muscular bodies. Both are expert horsemen and both have fond memories of their childhood spent at their ancestral home in Périgord.

When Julie receives an urgent call from d'Espi-

vant, who is critically ill, she accepts his invitation to
visit him. Slowly, in the course of their conversation
Julie's love for her cunning and still attractive ex-hus-
band is revived. At first she feels ill, which in the
world of Colette's healthy and vigorous women is a
premonitory symptom of love, "the amorous catastrophe."[36] When d'Espivant asks her to participate in a
blackmail scheme, she agrees, believing that her
former husband still finds her attractive. Once the
scheme succeeds, Julie realizes that d'Espivant neither
loves nor desires her. He does not even keep his part
of the bargain; shrewdly he arranges things in such a
way that all the moral onus of the scheme falls on her.
As Colette's heroines invariably do when they are hurt,
she stoically endures the humiliation and suffering
which, at least in Colette's fictional world, are the
inevitable consequences of love.

Colette's women never wallow in grief or self-
pity. "Once again I'm going to cure myself of Herbert,"[37] Julie says as she surveys the wreckage of her
life. Images of ruin and destruction appear with
increasing frequency throughout the second half of
the novel. Using a technique in which she was particularly adroit, Colette emphasizes the emotional state of
the protagonists by alluding discreetly to events in the
world around them; the action of *Julie de Carneilhan*
takes place in 1939 and in a France that would soon
be ravaged by war.

One sleepless night, Julie gets up, goes into the
kitchen and, seated under a naked lightbulb, begins
almost unconsciously to polish her riding boots. Her
seemingly meaningless act is the first manifestation of
an instinctual urge that prompts her to accompany
her brother Léon (who was no doubt modeled after

Colette's unmarried brother, Léo Colette, who died in 1940) back to their ancestral home.

Julie's and Léon's departure from Paris is the final scene of the novel, and it is an astonishing one, finely executed and charged with poetic beauty. It opens resoundingly with the ringing of an alarm clock and the neighing of horses. The hour is dawn, and Léon has arrived with the horses that he and Julie are going to ride back home. In quiet, remarkably understated prose, Colette evokes the early morning purity. But if the scene is bathed in limpid light, it is also tinged with sadness, for Julie is turning her back on love. Like most of Colette's heroines since Léa, Julie renounces the joys and sorrows of love, the somber, sulphurous world of sexual instincts, in short, the world that is represented by the constitutive symbol of Willy. The trip home, Léon tells her, may take "three weeks . . . three months . . . a life time."[38] Time, however, no longer matters. Eventually Julie will regain Paradise Lost, and there she will find peace.

In 1943 Colette published her last fictional work, *Gigi*, a collection of four short stories. Within the next few years, the title story was turned into both a highly successful stage play and a popular film, making it the most famous of Colette's works.

One of the characters in *Gigi* says of her aging sister: "She prefers living in a splendid past rather than in an ugly present."[39] This remark suggests the circumstances in which Colette wrote the story as well as the atmosphere of the story itself. It was written in 1942, a few months after Maurice Goudeket, Colette's third husband and constant companion, had been arrested by the Nazis and sent to a concentration camp. Moreover, Colette was by now completely bedridden with arthritis and often in great pain. But she continued to write newspaper articles in which she exhorted the women of France to avoid despair and cultivate hope, even happiness. *Gigi* should be seen in this light. It is a fairy tale of romance and happiness.

In *Gigi* Colette returns to the world in which her fiction first took shape—the world of the demi-monde in 1900. The milieu is one of elegant corruption, inhabited by women whose good taste and dignity are the result of strict adherence to the "honorable habits of women without honor."[40] Sixteen-year-old Gigi, Colette's final idealization of youthful exuberance and innocence, is being brought up by her grandmother and aunt, two aging courtesans. Bursting with life, the coltish Gigi is a restatement of the same ideal of youthfulness that Colette, some forty years before, had embodied in the figure of Claudine. The wealthy Gaston, who bears a marked resemblance to Renaud in *Claudine à Paris*, finds Gigi irresistible. When the young girl, to the great consternation of her grandmother and aunt, refuses Gaston's invitation to become his mistress, the love-sick suitor heroically proposes marriage.

The characters in *Gigi* are shallow. Like other imaginative writers who are preoccupied with their own past, Colette attached a perhaps excessive importance to a form of life already vanished. Although the novel is beautifully executed, the material from which it is fashioned is thin. Still, the conversations are witty and full of sparkling humor. In fact, instead of being a portrayal of love, Colette's last fictional work is essentially a comedy of manners performed by a cast of stereotyped characters. As is true of any good comedy of manners, *Gigi* is a triumph of style.

5

The Way
Back Home

As we have seen, Colette's major fiction is invariably fashioned around the subject of love. Her perception of love as a harsh, fatalistic force that tyranically dominates a woman's destiny has its origin in her experiences with Willy whose milieu is for her a symbol of deceit and impurity. Expelled from Willy's world around 1906, Colette strove at first to assert her independence. Like Renée Néré, she sought peace in activity, in vagabondage.

Beginning in the 1920s, Colette's fictional heroines are no longer vagabonds. Entrapped in the web of love, they tend to rise ultimately to a certain level of dignity either by renouncing love (if they are on the brink of old age) or by accepting their feminine nature. In either case, they transcend the world symbolized by Willy and approach a level of being symbolized by Sido. In 1949, looking back on *La Maison de Claudine*, 1922 (*My Mother's House*) and *Sido* (1929), the two books in which she first celebrated her mother, Colette wrote:

By continually laying aside and taking up again *La Maison de Claudine*, then *Sido*, both of which are written in the form of short sketches, I never abandoned the personage who little by little made her presence felt in all the rest of my work: my mother.[1]

La Maison de Claudine is not in any narrative sense related to the Claudine novels. No doubt Colette, as has often been noted, chose this title because of the commercial value of the name Claudine. She saw no reason to refrain from cashing in on the continued popularity of her early novels. Then too, in her very first novel she had already begun to fashion an ideal of childhood, several features of which were embodied in the figure of Claudine. There is, perhaps, a certain logic in using the name of Claudine for a further development of basically the same ideal, even though it is elaborated in a different register and with far greater mastery of the art of writing.

The structure of *La Maison de Claudine* has posed a problem for critics. The first edition consisted of thirty brief stories and sketches which had appeared in various newspapers from about 1912 to 1922. To many readers it seemed that Colette had simply bundled off to her publisher a collection of random pieces dealing more or less with her childhood. To complicate matters, in the definitive edition of 1930 she added five stories, inserting two of them in the middle of the volume and tacking the other three on to the end.

By and large, the thirty-five chapters are arranged in chronological order, the earliest being scenes from childhood, the later ones, evocations of adolescence and maturity. In the final chapters Colette, now a forty-nine-year-old mother, recedes into the background and her nine-year-old daughter, Bel-Gazou, becomes the central figure. On one level, *La Maison de Claudine* may thus be read as a series of sketches and anecdotes so arranged that they constitute a kind of fictionalized autobiography.

And yet this reading is not completely satisfactory. Certain chapters simply do not fit into a chronological pattern. Chapter 6, for example, relates an anecdote about Bel-Gazou which, if the book's structure were determined exclusively by chronology, should not appear until the end. Nor would it be accurate to say that the chapters are grouped according to themes, such as family, friends, nature, animals. Perplexed by the book's apparent lack of structure, many critics have affirmed that it was carelessly composed. They propogated the totally illogical notion that Colette, although she constructed her novels with utmost care, somehow lapsed into formlessness in her nonfictional works.

One critic, however, Louis Forestier, refused to accept this view.[2] He discerned in *La Maison de Claudine* a structure which considerably illuminates the book's meaning and helps to explain what most readers have sensed: that *La Maison de Claudine*, *La Naissance du jour* and *Sido* are key works, essential for an understanding of Colette. Indeed, they are the cornerstone of Colette's work.

Forestier groups the chapters of *La Maison de Claudine* as follows: in 1-5 Colette evokes the family in which she grew up; in 6-9 society, as represented by language, books, culture in general, politics and contact with others, intrudes on the family and tends to be opposed to it; in Chapter 10, Minet-Chéri discovers the consoling properties of nature and animals, of "the garden and the circle of animals" which are "inseparable from my mother";[3] in 11-20 the maturing Colette is confronted with life's problems—death, love, marriage, maternity, jealousy, deception. Strategically placed at the precise numerical center of *La Maison de Claudine* are Chapters 17, "La petite Bouilloux" (Bouilloux is the surname of the heroine), and 18, "La Toutouque" (Toutouque is the name of the bulldog in the story): the first deals with the theme of love, the second with the theme of sexuality, "the maleficent force that can transform the gentlest of creatures into a savage brute."[4] These chapters, which are of crucial importance in the economy of the work, treat the two subjects that are at the heart of Colette's entire literary opus.

The first twenty chapters represent, then, a

descent from the initial innocence of childhood into adult life. The house and the garden which are, according to Colette's description in the famous opening pages of *La Maison de Claudine*, sanctuaries of warmth and primordial silence, mark the beginning of her journey. Chapter 20, which recounts Colette's schoolgirl crush on her older brother's best friend, ends with a sentence that suggests the transition from childhood to womanhood: "He went toward the house without saying another word, and I experienced for the first time, mixed with the huge childish sorrow I felt in losing Maurice, the small disappointment of a woman who has just triumphed."[5]

In the remaining sixteen chapters, Colette explores avenues that might lead from distress to happiness. The book thus assumes the character of a quest. Imagination, morals, laughter, and sentiment are each explored, often in amusing anecdotes, as Colette searches for an ethic that will assuage her anxieties. Ultimately, the road forward turns out to be the road back. Little by little the ethic represented by Sido, who believed that anxiety and sadness were forms of depravity, becomes Colette's own.

In the final four chapters Colette is more or less assimilated with Sido who, for the reader, exists not so much as the author's mother, but as an idealized portrait of Colette herself. Indeed, Colette assumes the role of mother, and Bel-Gazou incarnates innocence. The image of Sido, emerging from the author's past, fuses with that of Bel-Gazou. Together they seem to provoke in Colette a sense of wonderment and a feeling of renewed contact with the world of innocence and joy. As Forestier puts it, Colette discovers that she can indeed possess a world which heretofore she had thought was accessible only to children: "a world that is pure and marvelous, that has retained its 'original blueness.' "[6]

However, the possession and enjoyment of this world are possible only in the absence of "the supreme intruder, desire,"[7] or, to use another of Colette's euphemisms for sex, "the brief and localized pleasures of love."[8] The renunciation of love and an intense, at times rapturous, communion with nature and animals are the principal subjects of *La Naissance du jour*, 1928 (*Break of Day*), perhaps the strangest, richest, and most poetic of Colette's works.

In 1927 Colette had agreed to write a novel for the publishing house of Flammarion. She reread all of Sido's letters, intending to extract from them a subject for her novel. Then early in July she went to Saint-Tropez and began working on the book. Two years before, her constant companion, Maurice Goudeket, had introduced her to Saint-Tropez, which in the 1920s was a sleepy little fishing village unknown to tourists. As her books and letters show, Colette had been deeply moved by the Mediterranean landscape, its limpidness and its austerity. The small house she had recently purchased near Saint-Tropez—a house she celebrates in her works under the name of La Treille Muscate—became the setting of her new book.

A considerable portion of *La Naissance du jour* is devoted to Sido's correspondence, together with Colette's comments on it, and to evocations of La Treille Muscate and the surrounding landscape. The book, which was supposed to be a novel, turned out to be a hybrid genre: about two-thirds of it consists of reminiscences and lyrical sketches couched in an autobiographical mode, for Colette, using her own name, is the principal character; only about one-third of the book could be called novelistic. Two themes appear over and over in Sido's letters and in Colette's lengthy commentaries on them: Sido's perfect harmony with the natural world, from which she receives "the passing benediction of joy," nullifying pain and old age; and the transcendence of sexuality—a transcendence exemplified by Sido. Early in *La Naissance du jour* Colette announces that "love, one of the great commonplaces of existence is slowly withdrawing from my life. Maternal instinct is another great commonplace. Once we've left these behind, we find that all the rest is gay, varied, abundant."[9] La Treille Muscate, with its small garden full of plants and animals, symbolizes "all the rest."

The novelistic portion of the book restates in quasi-fictional form the theme of the withdrawal of love from Colette's life. In several of the sketches which describe life at La Treille Muscate, Colette mentions friends such as Francis Carco and Dunoyer de Segonzac who summered in the vicinity and whom she occasionally met in town or on the beach. This small group of people is augmented by a number of fictional characters, one of whom is Vial, a man considerably younger than Colette. When the fictional Vial falls in love with the real Colette, the line between fiction and autobiography becomes considerably blurred.

The major scene between Vial and Colette is a conversation that begins in the early evening and extends through the night, ending at dawn. Although the setting is rather contrived, the conversation, together with the interior monologue that accompanies it, is a subtle and even dramatic presentation, first, of a woman's acceptance of the fact that she is growing old and, secondly, of her tender, even regretful rejection of the youthful love being offered her.

Just as *La Retraite sentimentale* was Colette's
farewell to youth, so *La Naissance du jour* is her farewell to the years of maturity. She has survived the
night and now, with a kind of hushed awe, watches
the new day dawn, knowing that "it is not too much
to be born and to create each day."[10] Colette's long
and vibrant old age, ushered in by *La Naissance du
jour*, moves serenely toward its conclusion, which is
the subject of her meditations in one of her last books,
L'Étoile Vesper (*The Evening Star*).

Colette did not envisage her renunciation of Vial's
love as an impoverishment; on the contrary, she saw
it as a means of enriching herself. "One possesses
through abstaining, and only through abstaining,"[11]
she notes. In his penetrating essay on Colette, Thierry
Maulnier affirms that *La Naissance du jour* contains
the clearest expression of the theme he considers to
be the key to Colette's work—"the contradictory
theme of renunciation and enrichment, of enrichment
through renunciation, the theme of the inevitable,
which is endured and at the same time overcome by
earnest reflection on oneself and by courageous reso-
luteness."[12]

While writing *La Naissance du jour*, Colette was
passionately in love with Maurice Goudeket who later
insisted that he was not the model for Vial. The fact
that Colette wrote a book in which she renounces love
while being at the same time in love once again is
not particularly surprising. At fifty-five she knew that
Goudeket would be the last man in her life, although
she could not have foreseen that he would be her
faithful "friend," as she calls him, for the next twenty-
six years.

La Naissance du jour is obviously not intended
to be a description of the external events of Colette's

life; rather, it records the working out of a moral position. "An age comes," Colette declares early in the book, "when a woman's only task is to enrich her own self."[13] Approaching old age, she was fully conscious of the fact that the treasure she sought lay within herself, deposited there years before by Sido.

For Colette, however, the desire to examine the moral and spiritual legacy which Sido had bequeathed her did not necessitate a physical withdrawal from the world. Indeed, she remained as active in the thirties as she had been in the twenties. In addition to writing, she gave numerous lectures in France, Germany, Switzerland, Belgium and North Africa. In 1932 she opened a beauty parlor in Paris—a project she had had in mind for some ten years. Many of Colette's contemporaries thought it unseemly that a writer of her stature should become a beautician. Colette's sole source of income, however, was her writing, and the Depression had seriously affected the publishing industry. Having a marked desire for security, comfort, and even a bit of luxury, Colette may well have felt it prudent to seek a second source of income. In any case, the venture was not a success and Colette's career as a beautician was short-lived.

Her interest in the theater had not waned. During the twenties she had returned to the stage to act in adaptations of *Chéri* and *La Vagabonde*. In the 1930s she served as drama critic for various newspapers and journals, often attending the theater four or five times a week. In addition, Colette and Goudeket accepted various journalistic assignments, which included covering the maiden voyage to New York of the luxury liner *Normandy*, and the sensational trial that followed the murder of several prostitutes in a North African brothel.

These were clearly active years in which Colette was sustained by the presence of Goudeket whose respect and adulation were no doubt a soothing anti-dote to Willy's bumptiousness and Jouvenel's indiffer-ence. At the same time, however, Colette pursued the literary task she had begun in *La Maison de Claudine* and *La Naissance du jour*—that of illuminating the figure of Sido which she knew to be at the source of her own being.

Indeed *Sido* (1929) represents a further attempt on the part of Colette to find herself by resurrecting the past—"the key that reopens childhood."[14] "It takes time for the absent to assume their true shape within us,"[15] she notes. Dividing the book into three sections —Sido, the Captain, the children—Colette explores her past, searching for that mysterious essence which she calls, putting it in quotation marks, "Sido." When, in other books, Colette refers to the real Sido, she writes her mother's name without quotation marks. In *Sido*, however, the name always appears as "Sido." Clearly, Colette is here referring, not to the real per-son, but to the idealized image that has taken shape within her.

Writing in 1949, Colette maintained that she had not yet discovered all the treasure her mother had deposited in her. Still, it might be argued that she would not have sought Sido if she had not already found her. Indeed, Colette's final years, as well as the joyful and beautifully serene books that bring her literary career to its quiet close, bear witness to the fact that she had discovered the secret of Sido's extraordinary sense of plenitude.

Ultimately, Sido's house and garden, to which Colette, the vagabond, returns, transcend the particu-lar house and garden in which Minet-Chéri grew up.

They become a state of mind independent of any precise geographical place or of any particular time. This capacity to transform any house, any room, any garden into an enchanted retreat, an asylum, a paradise regained, accounts for the remarkable tranquility that emanates from the books Colette wrote during her last twelve or fourteen years. Although the physical boundary of her world gradually shrank to the confines of her bed, which she called her "raft," she continued to cultivate her sense of wonderment, delighting in the beauty of a flower, the taste of an orange, or the presence of an old friend.

A sense of constant discovery illuminates two of Colette's last and greatest books, *L'Étoile Vesper*, 1946 (*The Evening Star*) and *Le Fanal bleu*, 1949 (*The Blue Lantern*). Both are journals in which Colette jots down thoughts, impressions and reminiscences in prose that is a model of simple elegance and pellucid beauty. The tiny world illuminated by her famous blue-shaded lamp becomes a paradise which the reader is invited to share. Possessing an extraordinary capacity for extracting beauty from ordinary things, Colette never ceased celebrating life in the face of old age, pain and death. Bedridden and approaching the age of eighty, she wrote:

I admire, I rejoice, I get around, I brush up against all those well-legged people and sing their praises. Oh no, oh no, do not for a moment think that I am jealous or sad! Do me the honor of believing that I know how to enjoy the portion I have left, to bear lightly what would have seemed heavy before, and to extract from this imperfection which, like a geological fault, wears me away and cuts into me—yes, I shall say it—a certain nobility.[16]

Viewed as a whole, Colette's work is curiously Janus-faced. The novels depict a world in which there is no communication between beings who, restless and sorrowful, are driven by forces they scarcely understand and cannot control. Beyond this turmoil, however, Colette posits another world, a world of radical innocence and beauty. Here Colette, who was completely indifferent to philosophical speculation, approaches the grand tradition of Platonism, for she shares with all thinkers of Platonic persuasion, the vision of an ideal country to which she aspires. Ultimately she becomes a poet who sings of the restitution of all things to their essential purity.

~~~~~~~~~~~~~~~~~~~~~~~~~~~~~~~~~~~~~

Notes

Unless otherwise indicated, all references are to the Fleuron edition of Colette's *Oeuvres complètes*, 15 volumes, Paris (Flammarion), 1948-50. Unfortunately, this edition is out-of-print. To replace it, Flammarion published in 1960 a three-volume edition of Colette's *Oeuvres*, which, however, is not complete. References to volume number and page number in the three-volume edition are indicated in parentheses. The excerpts cited are offered in my own translations.

1. The Beginning

1. *Sido*, VII, 197 (III, 269).
2. *L'Étoile Vesper*, XIII, 303 (III, 879).
3. *Le Képi*, XII, 249 (III, 686). In her article entitled "Balzac et Colette," *Revue d'Histoire Littéraire de la France*, Jan.-March 1960, Nicole Houssa declares that Colette's work contains allusions to fifty-five Balzacian characters.
4. Madeleine Raaphorst-Rousseau, *Colette, sa vie et son art* (Paris: Nizet, 1964), p. 29.
5. *Sido*, VII, 219 (III, 284).

6. *Journal à rebours*, XII, 80.
7. *Sido*, VII, 197, (III, 270).
8. *Journal à rebours*, XII, 97.
9. *La Naissance du jour*, VIII, 43 (II, 334).
10. *Mes Apprentissages*, XI, 33 (III, 396).
11. *Journal à rebours*, XII, 25.
12. Eliseo Vivas, *D. H. Lawrence: The Failure and the Triumph of Art* (Evanston, Ill.: Northwestern University Press, 1960). See chapter X and appendix.
13. *Mes Apprentissages*, XI, 54 (III, 409).
14. Ibid., XI, 26 (III, 392).
15. Ibid., XI, 35 (III, 397).
16. *Noces*, VII, 251.
17. Ibid., VII, 252.
18. Ibid., VII, 249.
19. *Mes Apprentissages*, XI, 35 (III, 397).
20. Ibid., XI, 22 (III, 389).
21. Ibid., XI, 57 (III, 411).

2. *Claudine*

1. *Claudine à l'école*, I, 15 (I, 7).
2. Ibid., I, 16 (I, 7).
3. *La Vagabonde*, IV, 27 (I, 716).
4. Claude Roy, *Descriptions critiques* (Paris: Gallimard, 1949), p. 113.
5. Anne A. Ketchum, *Colette ou la naissance du jour* (Paris: Minard, 1968), p. 15.
6. *Claudine à l'école*, I, 141-2 (I, 82).
7. For example, in the first story in *Le Pur et l'impur*, the aging Charlotte frequents an opium den where she makes love with her young lover, feigning orgasm to reassure the young man.
8. *Claudine à l'école*, I, 18 (I, 9).
9. Ibid., I, 100 (I, 56).
10. Ibid., I, 156-7 (I, 91).
11. Ibid., I, 149 (I, 86).

12. *Mes Apprentissages*, XI, 58 (III, 412).

13. *De ma Fenêtre*, XII, 345.

14. Peter Selz, *Art Nouveau* (New York: The Museum of Modern Art, 1960), p. 16.

15. *Discours de Réception à l'Académie Royale Belge*, XIII, 449.

16. Gide, *Journal*, (Paris: Gallimard, Pléiade, 1948), p. 1245, entry for March 8, 1936.

17. Quoted by Raaphorst-Rousseau, p. 64.

18. *Claudine à Paris*, I, 274 (I, 162).

19. *Le Pur et l'impur*, IX, 63 (III, 334).

20. *Claudine à Paris*, I, 444 (I, 268).

21. *Claudine en ménage*, II, 7 (I, 281).

22. Ibid., II, 15 (I, 286).

23. *L'Étoile Vesper*, XIII, 277 (III, 863).

24. *Claudine en ménage*, II, 47 (I, 305).

25. *Le Pur et l'impur*, IX, 51-2 (III, 327-8).

26. *Claudine en ménage*, II, 17 (I, 287).

27. *Le Pur et l'impur*, IX, 42-3 (III, 321-2).

28. *La Chatte*, IX, 210 (II, 522).

29. *Le Pur et l'impur*, IX, 26-7 (III, 312).

30. In *Duo*, IX, 329 (II, 595) Colette wrote: "Why is it that a man can never talk about a woman's sexual nature without making incredibly stupid remarks?"

31. *Claudine en ménage*, II, 70-1 (I, 321).

32. Ibid., II, 106 (I, 344).

33. *Le Pur et l'impur*, IX, 51 (III, 327).

34. *Claudine en ménage*, II, 55 (I, 311).

35. *La Vagabonde*, IV, 191 (I, 815).

36. *Claudine s'en va*, II, 231 (I, 421).

37. Ibid., II, 251 (I, 434).

38. Ibid., II, 333 (I, 486).

39. Ibid., II, 318 (I, 477).

40. *Mes Apprentissages*, XI, 59 (III, 412).

41. *Claudine s'en va*, II, 335 (I, 487).

42. Quoted by Raaphorst-Rousseau, pp. 204-5.

43. *De ma Fenêtre*, XII, 325.

44. *L'Étoile Vesper*, XIII, 305 (III, 880).

45. *La Maison de Claudine*, VII, 139-42 (III, 233-4).
46. *Mes Apprentissages*, XI, 68 (III, 418).

3. The Vagabond

1.   *Mes Apprentissages*, XI, 113 (III, 446).
2.   Ibid., XI, 125 (III, 453).
3.   *Bella-Vista*, XI, 197 (III, 494).
4.   *Mes Apprentissages*, XI, 81 (III, 426).
5.   *La Retraite sentimentale*, II, 354 (I, 500).
6.   Ibid., II, 381 (I, 517).
7.   *La Vagabonde*, IV, 197 (I, 819).
8.   *La Naissance du jour*, VIII, 126 (II, 383).
9.   *La Retraite sentimentale*, II, 348 (I, 496).
10. Ibid., II, 349 (I, 497).
11. Ibid., II, 484 (I, 578).
12. *Les Vrilles de la vigne*, III, 206.
13. Ibid., III, 212.
14. Ibid., III, 222.
15. Ibid., III, 223.
16. *Dialogues de bêtes*, III, 378-9 (II, 783).
17. *La Vagabonde*, IV, 10 (I, 705).
18. Ibid., IV, 10 (I, 705).
19. Ibid., IV, 10 (I, 705-6).
20. Ibid., IV, 13 (I, 707).
21. Ibid., IV, 18 (I, 711).
22. Ibid., IV, 50 (I, 730).
23. Ibid., IV, 65 (I, 739).
24. Ibid., IV, 114 (I, 768).
25. Ibid., IV, 127 (I, 775).
26. Ibid., IV, 161 (I, 796).
27. *Le Blé en herbe*, VII, 330 (II, 282).
28. *La Vagabonde*, IV, 150 (I, 790).
29. Ibid., IV, 180 (I, 808).
30. Ibid., IV, 189 (I, 814).
31. Ibid., IV, 193 (I, 817).
32. Ibid., IV, 220 (I, 834).

33. Ibid., IV, 222 (I, 835).
34. Ibid., IV, 223 (I, 836).
35. *L'Entrave*, IV, 336 (I, 905).
36. Ibid., IV, 360 (I, 920).
37. Ibid., IV, 371 (I, 927).
38. Ibid., IV, 380 (I, 933).
39. *La Vagabonde*, IV, 208 (I, 825).
40. *L'Étoile Vesper*, XIII, 325 (III, 892).
41. *L'Entrave*, IV, 403 (I, 947).
42. *L'Étoile Vesper*, XIII, 326 (I, 892).
43. Quoted by Claude Chauvière, *Colette* (Paris: Firmin-Didot et Compagnie, 1931), 146-8.
44. *Mitsou*, V, 211 (II, 60).
45. Ibid., V, 200 (II, 53). Similarly, in *Les Vrilles de la vigne*, III, 258, Colette describes a girl who suffers intensely when she is abandoned by her lover, but who bears up admirably under the strain: "A doll's heroism (héroïsme de poupée)," Colette notes, "but heroism all the same."

4. The Novels of Maturity

1. *Chéri*, VI, 13 (II, 63).
2. Ibid., VI, 13 (II, 63).
3. Ibid., VI, 142 (II, 142).
4. *L'Étoile Vesper*, XIII, 278 (III, 863).
5. *Chéri*, VI, 69 (II, 98).
6. *La Fin de Chéri*, VI, 268 (II, 220).
7. Ibid., VI, 188 (II, 171).
8. Ibid., VI, 205 (II, 182).
9. Ibid., VI, 217 (II, 189).
10. Ibid., VI, 224 (II, 193).
11. Ibid., VI, 179 (II, 166).
12. Ibid., VI, 243 (II, 205).
13. Ibid., VI, 254-6 (II, 212-3).
14. *La Naissance du jour*, VIII, 20 (II, 320).
15. *Le Blé en herbe*, VII, 256 (II, 233).

16.   Ibid., VII, 353 (II, 295).
17.   Ibid., VII, 324 (II, 277).
18.   Ibid., VII, 294 (II, 259).
19.   Ibid., VII, 372 (II, 307).
20.   *La Seconde*, VIII, 261 (II, 467).
21.   *La Chatte*, IX, 203 (II, 518).
22.   Ibid., IX, 193 (II, 512).
23.   *La Naissance du jour*, VIII, 53 (II, 340).
24.   *La Chatte*, IX, 239 (II, 539).
25.   Ibid., IX, 145 (II, 484).
26.   *Le Pur et l'impur*, IX, 24 (III, 310).
27.   *Journal à rebours*, XII, 44.
28.   *Duo*, IX, 282 (II, 566).
29.   Ibid., IX, 282 (II, 566).
30.   Ibid., IX, 274 (II, 562).
31.   Ibid., IX, 265 (II, 557).
32.   Ibid., IX, 342 (II, 603).
33.   Ibid., IX, 346 (II, 605).
34.   Ibid., IX, 337 (II, 600).
35.   Ibid., IX, 253 (II, 549).
36.   *La Naissance du jour*, VII, 56 (II, 342).
37.   *Julie de Carneilhan*, XI, 542 (II, 732).
38.   Ibid., XI, 546 (II, 735).
39.   *Gigi*, XIII, 16 (III, 708).
40.   Ibid., XIII, 28 (III, 715).

5. The Way Back Home

1.   *La Maison de Claudine*, VII, 7, preface written for the Fleuron edition.
2.   Louis Forestier, *Chemins vers "La Maison de Claudine" et "Sido"* (Paris: Société d'édition d'enseignement supérieur, 1968), p. 24.
3.   *La Maison de Claudine*, VII, 53 (III, 175).
4.   Ibid., VII, 98 (III, 204).
5.   Ibid., VII, 106 (III, 210).

6. Forestier, p. 31. Colette's expression, "original blue-ness," appears in *Sido*, VII, 181 (III, 260).

7. *La Naissance du jour*, VIII, 89 (II, 361).

8. Ibid., VIII, 13 (II, 315).

9. Ibid., VIII, 18 (II, 319).

10. Ibid., VIII, 125 (II, 383).

11. Ibid., VIII, 24 (II, 323).

12. Thierry Maulnier, *Introduction à Colette* (Paris: La Palme, 1954), pp. 40-1.

13. *La Naissance du jour*, VIII, 33 (II, 328).

14. *Journal à rebours*, XII, 96.

15. *Sido*, VII, 209-10 (III, 278).

16. *Le Fanal bleu*, XIV, 29 (III, 912).

~~~~~~

Bibliography

I. Colette's Works

PRINCIPAL WORKS

The Roman numeral at the end of each entry indicates in which volume of the Fleuron edition that entry may be found.

Claudine à l'école. Paris: P. Ollendorf, 1900. (*Claudine at School,* tr. Antonia White. London: Secker and Warburg, 1956; New York: Farrar, Straus and Cudahy, 1957.) I

Claudine à Paris. Paris: P. Ollendorf, 1901. (*Claudine in Paris,* tr. Antonia White. New York: Farrar, Straus and Cudahy, 1958.) I

Claudine en ménage. Paris: P. Ollendorf, 1902. (*The Indulgent Husband,* tr. Frederick A. Blossom. New York: Rinehart and Co., 1935; *Claudine Married,* tr. Antonia White. New York: Farrar, Straus and Cudahy, 1960.) II

Claudine s'en va. Paris: P. Ollendorf, 1903. (*The Innocent Wife,* tr. Frederick A. Blossom. New York: Farrar and Rinehart, 1934; *Claudine and Annie,* tr. Antonia White. London: Secker and Warburg, 1962.) II

Dialogues de bêtes. Paris: Mercure de France, 1904. (*Crea-
    tures Great and Small,* tr. Enid McLeod. New York:
    Farrar, Straus and Cudahy, 1957.) III
La Retraite sentimentale. Paris: Mercure de France, 1907.
    II
Les Vrilles de la vigne. Paris: Editions de la Vie Parisienne,
    1908. III
L'Ingénue libertine. Paris: P. Ollendorf, 1909. (*The Gentle
    Libertine,* tr. R.C.B. New York: Farrar and Rinehart,
    1931; *The Innocent Libertine,* tr. Antonia White.
    London: Secker and Warburg, 1968.) III
La Vagabonde. Paris: P. Ollendorf, 1911. (*The Vagabond,*
    tr. Enid McLeod. New York: Farrar, Straus and
    Young, 1955.) IV
L'Envers du music-hall. Paris: Flammarion, 1913. (*Music-
    Hall Sidelights,* tr. Anne-Marie Callimachi. New York:
    Farrar, Straus and Cudahy, 1958.) V
L'Entrave. Paris: Librairie des lettres, 1913. (*Recaptured,*
    tr. Viola Gerard Garvin. New York: Cosmopolitan
    Book Corporation, 1931; *The Shackle,* tr. Antonia
    White. London: Secker and Warburg, 1964.) IV
La Paix chez les bêtes. Paris: A. Fayard, 1916. V
Les Heures longues. Paris: A. Fayard, 1917. V
Mitsou ou comment l'esprit vient aux filles. Paris: A. Fay-
    ard, 1919. (*Mitsou,* tr. Raymond Postgate. New York:
    Farrar, Straus and Cudahy, 1958.) V
Chéri. Paris: A. Fayard, 1920. (*Chéri and The Last of
    Chéri,* tr. Roger Senhouse. New York: Farrar, Straus
    and Young, 1953.) VI
La Maison de Claudine. Paris: J. Ferenczi, 1922. (*My
    Mother's House and Sido,* tr. Enid McLeod and Una
    Troubridge. New York: Farrar, Straus and Young,
    1953.) VII
Le Voyage égoïste. Paris: Edouard Pelletan, 1922. VI
Le Blé en herbe. Paris: Flammarion, 1923. (*Ripening Seed,*
    tr. Roger Senhouse. New York: Farrar, Straus and
    Cudahy, 1956.) VII
La Femme cachée. Paris: Flammarion, 1924. VII

Aventures quotidiennes. Paris: Flammarion, 1924. VI

L'Enfant et les sortilèges. Musique de Maurice Ravel. Paris: Durand et Cie., 1925. (*The Boy and the Magic,* tr. Christopher Fry. New York: Putnam, 1965.) XV

La Fin de Chéri. Paris: Flammarion, 1926. (*Chéri and The Last of Chéri,* tr. Roger Senhouse. New York: Farrar, Straus and Young, 1953.) VI

La Naissance du jour. Paris: Flammarion, 1928. (*A Lesson in Love,* tr. Rosemary Benêt. New York: Farrar and Rinehart, 1932; *Break of Day,* tr. Enid McLeod. New York: Farrar, Straus and Cudahy, 1961.) VIII

La Seconde. Paris: J. Ferenczi, 1929. (*The Other One,* tr. Viola Gerard Garvin. New York: Cosmopolitan Book Corporation, 1931.) VIII

Sido. Paris: Editions Krâ, 1929. (*My Mother's House and Sido,* tr. Enid McLeod and Una Troubridge. New York: Farrar, Straus and Young, 1953.) VII

Douze Dialogues de bêtes. Paris: Mercure de France, 1930. (*Creatures Great and Small,* tr. Enid McLeod. New York: Farrar, Straus and Cudahy, 1957.) III

Paradis terrestres. Lausanne: Gonin et Cie., 1932. VIII

Prisons et Paradis. Paris: J. Ferenczi, 1932. VIII

Le Pur et l'impur (entitled *Ces Plaisirs . . .* in the first edition). Paris: J. Ferenczi, 1932. (*The Pure and the Impure,* tr. Herma Briffault. New York: Farrar, Straus and Giroux, 1967.) IX

La Chatte. Paris: Grasset, 1933. (*The Cat,* tr. Antonia White. London: Secker and Warburg, 1953; in *7 by Colette,* New York: Farrar, Straus and Cudahy, 1955.) IX

Duo. Paris: J. Ferenczi, 1934. (*The Married Lover,* tr. Marjorie Laurie. London: Werner Laurie, 1935; *Duo,* tr. Frederick A. Blossom. New York: Farrar and Rinehart, 1935.) IX

Mes Apprentissages. Paris: J. Ferenczi, 1936. (*My Apprenticeship,* tr. Helen Beauclerk. London: Secker and Warburg, 1957.) XI

Bella-Vista. Paris: J. Ferenczi, 1937. (In *The Tender Shoot*

and Other Stories, tr. Antonia White. New York:
    Farrar, Straus and Cudahy, 1959.) XI

Le Toutounier. Paris: J. Ferenczi, 1939. IX

Chambre d'hôtel. Paris: A. Fayard, 1940. (*Chance Ac-
    quaintances*, tr. Patrick Leigh Fermor, in *7 by Colette*.
    New York: Farrar, Straus and Cudahy, 1955.) XI

Journal à rebours. Paris: A. Fayard, 1941. XII

Julie de Carneilhan. Paris: A. Fayard, 1941. (*Julie de
    Carneilhan*, tr. Patrick Leigh Fermor, in *Gigi, Chance
    Acquaintances and Julie de Carneilhan*. New York:
    Farrar, Straus and Cudahy, 1952.) XI

De ma Fenêtre. Paris: Aux Armes de France, 1942. XII

Le Képi. Paris: A. Fayard, 1943. ("The Kepi," tr. Antonia
    White, in *The Tender Shoot and Other Stories*. New
    York: Farrar, Straus and Cudahy, 1959.) XII

Gigi et autres nouvelles. Lausanne: La Guilde du Livre,
    1944. (*Gigi*, tr. Roger Senhouse, in *Gigi, Chance Ac-
    quaintances and Julie de Carneilhan*. New York:
    Farrar, Straus and Cudahy, 1952.) XIII

Trois . . . Six . . . Neuf . . . Paris: Corrêa, 1944. XII

Belles Saisons. Paris: Éditions de la Galerie Charpentier,
    1945. IX

L'Étoile Vesper. Geneva: Éditions du Milieu du Monde,
    1946. (*The Evening Star*, tr. David Le Vay. London:
    Peter Owen Ltd., 1973.) XIII

Pour un herbier. Lausanne: Mermod, 1948. XIV

Trait pour Trait. Paris: Éditions Le Fleuron, 1949. XIV

Journal intermittent. Paris: Éditions Le Fleuron, 1949. XIV

Le Fanal bleu. Paris: J. Ferenczi, 1949. (*The Blue Lantern*,
    tr. Roger Senhouse. New York: Farrar, Straus and Co.,
    1963.) XIV

La Fleur de l'âge. Paris: Éditions Le Fleuron, 1949. XIV

En Pays connu. Paris: Éditions Manuel Bruker, 1949. XIV

PUBLISHED CORRESPONDENCE

*Une Amitié inattendu. Correspondance de Colette et de
    Francis Jammes*. Paris: Émile-Paul Frères, 1945.

Lettres à Hélène Picard. Paris: Flammarion, 1958.

Lettres à Marguerite Moreno. Paris: Flammarion, 1959.
Lettres de la Vagabonde. Paris: Flammarion, 1961.
Lettres au Petit Corsaire. Paris: Flammarion, 1963.
Lettres à ses pairs. Correspondance inédite de Colette à Marcel Proust, Alfred Jarry, Paul Léautaud, etc. Paris: Flammarion, 1973.

VOLUMES CONTAINING SELECTED PASSAGES
FROM COLETTE'S WORKS

Colette. Earthly Paradise: An Autobiography drawn from her lifetime writings, ed. Robert Phelps. New York: Farrar, Straus and Giroux, 1966. Also published in French as *Autobiographie tirées des oeuvres de Colette.* Paris: A. Fayard, 1966.
Places. Collection of passages from *Trois . . . six . . . neuf . . . , En Pays connu, Prisons et Paradis, Paysages et Portraits, Journal intermittent.* Tr. David Le Vay. London: Peter Owen Ltd., 1970.
Contes des mille et un matins. Collection of articles Colette wrote for the newspaper *Le Matin.* Paris: Flammarion, 1970. Published in English as *The Thousand and One Mornings,* tr. Margaret Crosland and David Le Vay. London: Peter Owen Ltd., 1973.

II. Works on Colette

Beaumont, Germaine. "Présentation," *Colette par elle-même.* Paris: Éditions du Seuil, 1956, 5-50.
Brasillach, Robert. "Colette ou la Sagesse de Sido," in *Portraits.* Paris: Plon, 1935.
Chauvière, Claude. *Colette.* Paris: Firmin-Didot, 1931.
Cocteau, Jean. *Colette.* Paris: Grasset, 1955.
Crosland, Margaret. *Madame Colette. A Provincial in Paris.* London: Peter Owen Ltd., 1953.
———. *Colette: The Difficulty of Loving.* London: Peter Owen Ltd., 1973.

Davies, Margaret. *Colette*. Edinburgh and London: Oliver and Boyd, 1961.

Desonay, Fernand. "Quelques thèmes d'inspiration chez Colette," *Bulletin de l'Académie Royale de Langue et de Littérature française de Belgique*, XXXII (1954), 125-40.

Fillon, Amélie. *Colette*. Paris: Éditions de la Caravelle, 1953.

Fischler, A. "Unity in Colette's *Le Blé en herbe*," *Modern Language Quarterly*, XXX (1969), 248-64.

Forestier, Louis. *Chemins vers "La Maison de Claudine" et "Sido."* Paris: Société d'édition d'enseignement supérieur, 1968.

Gandon, Yves. "Colette ou la sainteté du style," in *Le Démon du style*. Paris: Plon, 1938.

Goudeket, Maurice. *Près de Colette*. Paris: Flammarion, 1956. (*Close to Colette*. Tr. Enid McLeod. New York: Farrar, Straus and Cudahy, 1957.)

———. "Colette et l'art d'écrire," lecture given in April 1959, *Extraits des Annales de la Faculté des Lettres et Sciences Humaines d'Aix*, XXXIII.

———. *La Douceur de vieillir*. Paris: Flammarion, 1965.

Houssa, Nicole. *Le Souci de l'expression chez Colette*. Brussels: Palais des Académies, 1958.

Ketchum, Anne A. *Colette ou la naissance du jour—étude d'un malentendu*. Paris: Minard (Lettres Modernes), 1968.

Larnac, Jean. *Colette, sa vie, son oeuvre*. Paris: Simon Krâ, 1927.

Le Hardouin, Maria. *Colette*. Paris: Éditions Universitaires, 1956.

Marks, Elaine. *Colette*. New Brunswick, New Jersey: Rutgers University Press, 1960.

Maulnier, Thierry. *Introduction à Colette*. Paris: La Palme, 1954.

Mudrick, Marvin. "Colette, Claudine and Willy," *Hudson Review*, XVI (1963), 559-72.

Olken, I. T. "Aspects of Imagery in Colette: Color and Light," P.M.L.A., LXXVII (March, 1962), 140-48.

————. "Imagery in *Chéri* and *La Fin de Chéri*," *Studies in Philology*, LX (1963), 96-115.

Raaphorst-Rousseau, Madeleine. *Colette, sa vie et son art.* Paris: Nizet, 1964.

Reboux, Paul. *Colette ou le génie du style.* Paris: Rasmussen, 1925.

Roy, Claude. *Descriptions critiques.* Paris: Gallimard, 1949, 107-18.

Trahard, Pierre. *L'Art de Colette.* Paris: Jean Renard, 1941.

Truc, Gonzague. *Madame Colette.* Paris: Corrêa, 1941.

Index

Index

149